Performance Management in Local Government

Managing Local Government Series

Financial Management in Local Government (second edition)
by David Rawlinson and Brian Tanner

Human Resource Management in Local Government (second edition)
by Alan Fowler

Public Relations in Local Government
by David Walker

Renewing Public Management: an agenda for local governance
by Michael Clarke

Shaping Organisational Cultures in Local Government
by Janet Newman

Understanding the Management of Local Government: its special purposes, conditions and tasks (second edition) by John Stewart

Performance Management in Local Government

The Route to Best Value

SECOND EDITION

Steve Rogers

This book is for Carolyn. Her love and support, and her help in producing the manuscript, made it possible.

FINANCIAL TIMES
MANAGEMENT

LONDON · SAN FRANCISCO
KUALA LUMPUR · JOHANNESBURG

Financial Times Management delivers the knowledge, skills and understanding that enable students, managers and organisations to achieve their ambitions, whatever their needs, wherever they are.

London Office:
128 Long Acre, London WC2E 9AN
Tel: +44 (0)171 447 2000
Fax: +44 (0)171 240 5771
Website: www.ftmanagement.com

A Division of Financial Times Professional Limited

First published in Great Britain 1990
This edition published 1999

ISBN 0 273 61932 2

British Library Cataloguing in Publication Data
A CIP catalogue record for this book can be obtained from the British Library.

10 9 8 7 6 5 4 3 2 1

Typeset by Pantek Arts, Maidstone, Kent.
Printed and bound in Great Britain by Redwood Books, Trowbridge, Wiltshire.

The Publishers' policy is to use paper manufactured from sustainable forests.

Contents

Editors' foreword

This book is one of a series of management handbooks published by Financial Times Pitman Publishing in association with the Institute of Local Government Studies in the School of Public Policy at the University of Birmingham. The series is designed to help those concerned with management in local government to meet the challenge of the late 1990s. It is based on the belief that no period has been so important for local authorities to have effective management, responsive to both citizen and customer.

The mid-1990s have brought reorganisation to local authorities in Scotland, Wales and parts of England. No local authority, however, can escape the need to keep under continuous review its political and managerial structures and processes. All councils are caught up in far-reaching changes. Some of these come from local determination and decision, others from central government policy and yet others from deeper changes in society. New problems, issues and opportunities demand from local governments a capacity to respond in new ways. They have to become closer to their local communities, their public and the wide range of institutions and organisations involved in the governance of localities; they need to find imaginative solutions to the ever more complex problems of public policy; they have to manage their resources to achieve value for money and value in the services they provide; and they have to achieve effective management in all their activities. These are formidable challenges for the managers – and the politicians – involved.

There are plenty of management books, but this series is distinct. Its starting point is the need for emphasis on developing effective management in local government, associated with the need to take account of the particular nature of local government. The series sets out to be succinct and to be useful in the practical day-to-day world as well as being designed to be used as a prompt to management improvement.

In no sense are we pretending that this or other books in the series will show a *single way* to manage the local authority. Management is not like that. Our intention is to explore ideas and questions in order to help fashion the most helpful and effective approach to the local situation. We believe that local authority politicians and managers should draw on as wide a range of experience as possible but that this should be set in the context of the special purposes, conditions and tasks of local government. We hope that this book contributes to that end.

Professor Michael Clarke, Head of School of Public Policy,
University of Birmingham

Professor John Stewart, Institute of Local Government Studies
in the School of Public Policy, University of Birmingham

Preface

In writing this second edition I was faced with the choice of updating the first one or starting again from scratch. In opting for the latter, I was influenced not just by the limitations of the first edition but by the degree of change which has taken place in local government in the intervening eight years.

Local government is currently, yet again, being challenged for the way in which it manages itself internally and for its performance in producing local services. In that sense nothing has changed. But, despite the many challenges and criticisms, in reality much has changed in many local authorities. At the time of writing the first edition, performance management was a relatively new concept for many councillors and managers. Now it has become almost the norm – although the details of its practice remain variable. Many of the changes in performance management have resulted from local authorities' determination to improve on some of the earlier and cruder models and in many cases these improvements have been achieved by integrating ideas drawn from other schools of management.

This book is not intended as a 'how to do it' manual. While I hope it contains sufficient information to help those councillors and managers who wish to improve the way they manage performance, I have also adopted a critical stance to the topic. In some of its manifestations, performance management has been used as a rather blunt – even brutal – style of management which has achieved variable degrees of success. But there have also been many success stories and I anticipate there will be many more in the future.

There are a number of key messages in this book of which the most important is that performance management must be an *integrated* process that includes individual and organisational performance, that involves councillors as well as staff, and that creates a focus on effectiveness and quality as well as economy and efficiency.

Steve Rogers
Birmingham

1

What is Performance Management?

Introduction

Society needs its public service organisations to perform – to create policies and services that are effective in meeting local needs. In order to maximise their ability to produce the required performance, according to whatever criteria of performance society sets for them, these organisations need to be aware of the appropriate political and managerial processes. Because the performance of our public service institutions has been the subject of so much criticism, Performance Management has been invented and has occupied a central position in the radical reforms that have swept through the public sector during the last two decades.

For some managers in local government, and indeed for some politicians in central as well as local government, 'performance' appears to have achieved an almost magical significance, and has led to the creation not just of Performance Management but also performance reviews, performance audits, performance plans and performance appraisals. Imposing key performance targets and pledges, criticising organisational or individual performance, requiring a review or scrutiny of performance, publishing performance indicators, calling in auditors or inspectors to examine and pronounce on performance and requiring the production and implementation of performance improvement plans – all these procedures have increasingly become the norm rather than the exception. And, to some extent, many of these approaches do seem to have worked. Public services have changed and improved. Political and managerial decision making has become more focused on performance issues. Staff are more aware of the need to produce higher quality public services.

But within Performance Management lies an uneasy and often unreconciled conflict of assumptions. One set of assumptions is based around the need to

impose performance requirements, both within and from outside the organisation, while the other is based on the concept of **self-management and development** as the route to performance improvement. The gradual development of Performance Management over the last two decades may be seen either as an attempt to effect some reconciliation between these two sets of assumptions or as resulting from the shifting dominance of one set of assumptions over the other. Conflict has also resulted from the way in which Performance Management has been used either to produce real changes in performance or to create the image, and sometimes the illusion, of improvement.

Whatever the inherent conflicts, it is still necessary to determine whether Performance Management has magical properties. It does not. The Audit Commission, an important promulgator of Performance Management in local government, recognises that: 'There is nothing mystical about PM and it is not a universal panacea.' (Audit Commission, 1995a). But the Commission does acknowledge that:

> *Recently, PM has become something of an industry in its own right, dominated by 'industry experts' and management consultancies. It has been variously presented as a management theory, a fad and, by the committed, almost a theology. (Audit Commission, 1995a)*

Nonetheless, listening to the statements of some national and local politicians, civil servants and local managers, there apparently are some people for whom Performance Management is, if not quite magical, at least a ready-made and simple solution to many of their political or managerial problems.

Defining Performance Management

In moving towards a definition of Performance Management it is important for the reader to recognise that PM may be viewed narrowly as a set of tools and techniques which can be used by managers and politicians to manage performance within their own organisations, or it can be viewed more widely as a pattern of thinking that results from a wide-ranging set of changing political, economic, social and ethical pressures that have impacted on local authorities in ways that are far more extensive than simply the deployment of specific techniques. In this broader context, Performance Management is not just a process for ensuring that public service organisations and their employees are well placed to produce the performance which society requires of them, it is also part of the process by which performance itself is defined, by which criteria of performance are established and by which societal, political and managerial judgements are made of those who are performing. Performance Management creates the performance required of local authorities – it does not just ensure that local authorities are well enough managed to produce the required performance.

In its crudest manifestation, Performance Management can be summarised as an approach which is based on just four basic principles.

- Management by **objective**.
- Management by **accountability**.
- Management by **number**.
- Management by **reward and punishment**.

Put simply, the theory requires you to:

- determine, express and communicate objectives for all parts of the organisation;
- design the organisation so that it, and its individual employees, can be held accountable through processes for monitoring and reviewing performance;
- express all objectives in quantitative form, using performance targets, standards, indicators and measures;
- utilise appropriate reward and punishment mechanisms to induce individuals and organisations to behave in a manner that enables the organisation, and the wider political process, to achieve their objectives.

At this point some readers, particularly those who have worked diligently and effectively to make Performance Management a dynamic, realistic and useful force in their organisation, will have thrown up their hands in horror at the message they have just read. They will know that Performance Management cannot be contained in such a simplistic and crude definition. But other readers – and this is the worrying aspect – will recognise that definition as corresponding to their experience of Performance Management – a crude and simplistic approach to the management of organisations and people.

The definition may be crude and simplistic in its brevity but is it wrong? There is an undeniable strength and relevance to these basic concepts. There is plenty of practical and experimental evidence to demonstrate that individuals and organisations need a sense of purpose expressed in clear objectives and targets in order to be effective. It is both helpful and necessary to quantify what is being done, what that 'doing' has achieved and what resources have been used in doing it. There is also plenty of evidence that individuals respond positively to certain kinds of incentives and rewards and that they also respond, but not always in a predictable way, to criticism and punishment. So the basic concepts may not be wrong in an absolute sense. But, what those people who have initiated and facilitated the implementation of more successful Performance Management processes have learned, is that the basic concepts need to be interpreted and used with a sophisticated understanding of the values that underpin them, of the way they can be integrated, of the need to acknowledge and resolve the inherent conflicts, and of the need to ensure they are applied within a clear set of ethical rules and principles. Performance Management, like any approach to management – can be implemented well or badly. It can be used to create short-term results or it can be used to create the conditions for longer-term development and improvement. It can be applied ethically or unethically.

Developing a definition of Performance Management

In developing a more rounded definition of Performance Management it is helpful to consider some definitions which have been developed elsewhere. Six definitions will be explored, some drawn from local government and others from a wider context.

1 The Local Government Management Board

In 1993 the Local Government Management Board (LGMB) published a very useful guide to Performance Management. This definition is taken from Chapter 2 of the report:

> *Performance management links the strategy and service objectives of the authority to jobs and people. It is a systematic approach to managing effectively. Approaches vary in degree of formal structure. Its most detailed form is based on: setting corporate, service, team and individual objectives; recognising achievement; identifying training and development needs; and then using the knowledge gained to modify objectives and methods as necessary.*
>
> *Its prime aims are to improve performance and motivate staff by concentrating on priority objectives, raising commitment and releasing potential. It should be people rather than systems dominated and firmly within the strategy and direction set by elected members. With proper care in development, introduction and operation it will work, but will take time and effort. It should, however, be tied in with other service management and human resources policies, such as service planning and training and development. In addition, employers have the option of relating PM to their reward strategies. (LGMB (1993))*

There are several interesting points about this definition. Not surprisingly, given the general mission of the LGMB, there is a clear emphasis on the fact that organisational performance is a product of what people in the organisation do and achieve. There is also the acknowledgement that

Performance Management must be integrated with other processes in the local authority. In addition, there are some key words which will be repeated in other definitions – strategy; objectives; systematic, corporate; service; individual; recognition; reward; training; and development.

2 The Audit Commission

The Audit Commission has produced an extensive list of papers and reports on different aspects of Performance Management. It has also carried out many investigations into value for money and good management and, because of its role, has played a major part in determining the criteria by which the performance of local authorities has been judged in recent years. Its views on Performance Management are, as a consequence, both important and illuminating. Judging from two of its more recent publications on Performance Management (Audit Commission, 1995a and 1995b) its definition appears to centre on the phrase 'specify, communicate and evaluate aims and objectives at all levels'.

- *Specification* is referred to as 'the heart of the system – a set of aims for the organisation which are translated into specific objectives for each employee'.
- *Communication* is viewed in two ways: external communication, which 'lets managers amend objectives in response to the public needs'; and internal communication which 'allows staff to know their own responsibilities and influence detailed policy formulation.'
- *Evaluation* is regarded as 'Performance review' which 'tracks the performance of departments and service units and identifies actions necessary for improvement' and as 'Personal appraisal' for the individual employee. (Audit Commission, 1995a)

These three elements are identified in different terms as follows.

(i) *In order to maximise performance focus the efforts of the organisation on explicit, challenging and realistic aims and objectives.*
(ii) *Target and improve the understanding, commitment and contribution of individual staff in the delivery of those objectives.*
(iii) *Support the delegation of responsibility to front-line staff by using management by objectives.*
(iv) *Provide quantitative and qualitative standards for judging individual and organisational performance.*
(v) *Provide feedback to the organisation and to individual staff about their actual performance.*
(vi) *Identify and implement training and other actions necessary to improve individual performance. (Audit Commission, 1995a)*

The Management Handbook expresses the 'structure' of Performance Management in terms of six functions (Aims and objectives, Business planning, External communication, Internal communication, Performance review and Performance appraisal), combined into a 'strategy' consisting of the three processes referred to above (Specification, Communication and Evaluation), which is integrated with wider policies for paybill and personnel management. (Audit Commission, 1995b).

While the Audit Commission framework may differ from that of the LGMB it is fairly clear that similar terminology and concepts are being used. It should, however, be noted that the Audit Commission makes no explicit reference to elected members.

3 The Institute of Personnel Management

The Institute of Personnel Management's (IPM) research (1992) found that definitions of Performance Management and the actual systems used varied significantly in the 794 public and private sector organisations it surveyed but concluded that formal, integrated systems of Performance Management were likely to have the following characteristics.

- Mission statements that are communicated to all employees.
- Regularly communicated information on business plans.
- Implemented policies for such processes as total quality management and performance related pay.
- A focus on the performance of senior managers rather than other employees.
- Performance targets expressed in terms of measurable outputs, accountabilities and training targets.
- Formal appraisal processes and presentations by senior managers used as ways of communicating performance requirements.
- Performance requirements set on a regular basis.
- Performance requirements linked to pay, particularly for senior managers. (IPM, 1992).

The Institute also found that, as had been reported by other commentators, there were two broadly different approaches to Performance Management. The most common was a reward driven strategy which emphasised the role of performance related pay. The less common but, the Institute concluded, potentially more important and successful strategy was 'development driven integration' which emphasises the importance of a co-ordinated set of human resource strategies and activities.

4 A private sector definition

There are many definitions of Performance Management in the private sector. The following statement of aims is drawn from one writer who has written extensively on the topic.

Performance management aims to:

- *Achieve sustainable improvement in organisational performance.*
- *Enable individuals to develop their abilities, increase their job satisfaction and achieve their full potential, for their own benefit and for the benefit of the organisation as a whole.*
- *Develop constructive and open relationships between individuals and their managers in a process of continuing dialogue.*
- *Provide a framework for the agreement of objectives as expressed in targets and standards of performance so that mutual understanding of these objectives is increased.*
- *Provide for the accurate and objective measurement and assessment of performance in relation to agreed targets and standards so that individuals receive feedback from managers on how well they are doing.*
- *Enable individuals, with their managers, to agree improvement plans, methods of implementing them and jointly review training and development needs.*
- *Provide an opportunity for individuals to express their aspirations and concerns about their work.*
- *Provide a basis for rewarding people in relation to their contribution by financial and/or non-financial means. (Armstrong, 1993)*

While this statement places considerable importance on the development of dialogue, understanding and agreement between managers and their staff it is also clear that this has to be done while retaining the primary aim of improving organisational performance. Armstrong describes Performance Management as 'a systematic process of management, the overall aim of which is to increase organisational effectiveness by improving the performance of individuals and teams' and suggests that a 'textbook approach' to Performance Management has the following features:

- *A shared vision of organisational objectives communicated to all employees.*
- *Performance targets for each employee.*
- *Regular, formal processes for reviewing progress.*
- *The use of the review process to identify training and development outcomes.*
- *The use of the review process to determine reward outcomes.*
- *The evaluation of the whole process in terms of its contribution to organisational performance and to stimulate changes and developments in the process. (Armstrong, 1993)*

5 A consultant's definition

Guy Hollis, a partner in Coopers and Lybrand, presents Performance Management in the specific context of restructuring and renewing local government as a process that should operate at two levels – the organisational and the individual. At the organisational level:

> *it is concerned with ensuring that the (following) main factors affecting individual performance are complementary:*
>
> - *clearly stated goals and objectives;*
> - *human resource planning – pay and grading systems;*
> - *staff appraisal and development;*
> - *skills training. (Hollis, 1994)*

At the individual level, Hollis suggests that Performance Management involves regular reviews of performance and potential, planning for future development and reviews of the key factors such as pay and conditions that assist motivation.

6 A public sector management textbook definition

Writing in the context of public sector management, Nutley and Osborne (1994) suggest that 'rational' models of decision making, of which Performance Management is one manifestation, are often used in the public sector because of the difficulty experienced in trying to manage performance in organisations that are complex and have multiple objectives. While highlighting the limitations of the 'rational' model, Nutley and Osborne define Performance Management as:

> *... the evaluative process by which a view is reached about the performance of a set of activities measured against the achievement of specified objectives.*

Such a process, they maintain, contains the following elements.

- *Performance appraisal* of activities and programmes but not, surprisingly, of staff which is viewed as a separate aspect of 'the personnel systems of the organisation'.
- *Performance monitoring* – 'the ongoing assessment of a programme'.
- *Performance (ex-post) evaluation* – 'the retrospective evaluation of a programme against its objectives.'

- *Performance indicators* – both quantitative and qualitative 'surrogates for the levels of performance'.

Nutley and Osborne also define Performance Management as an overall process for ensuring that performance assessment is an integral part of all programmes, that it is understandable, that assessment informs all levels of planning and implementation and that such assessment enables performance improvement. Their focus on assessment and measurement, rather than on a process of actively *managing* performance, is characteristic of a particular view of Performance Management existing in the public sector. This view arises more from a public policy analysis perspective than that of public service management – a perspective that has led to the prominence of performance indicators as a main tool of Performance Management in the public sector.

A definition for today

In the first edition of this book, published in 1990, Performance Management was defined in the Preface as:

> *the interrelated processes which ensure that:*
>
> - *all the activities and people in a local authority contribute as effectively as possible to its objectives;*
> - *all activities and objectives are systematically reviewed in a way which enables a local authority to learn and thereby to improve its services to the community. (Rogers, 1990)*

Looked at eight years later one is struck by its generality and lack of precision. Perhaps its only merit lay in the introduction of the concept of 'learning' – a concept that is not made explicit in any of the above definitions and which the author remains convinced must lie at the heart of any formulation of Performance Management that will be of long-term benefit to a local authority and to its employees, service users and citizens.

In attempting to define Performance Management in a way that has contemporary significance for local authorities it is important to locate it within the contextual circumstances of local government.

For example:

- A local authority is an institution of government and not an agent of government. The concept of performance used in relation to local authorities must include the act of governing locally as well as the act of managing and administering the delivery of public services.

- Local councillors must, as a consequence, have a clear role in Performance Management. It is they who determine policies, priorities and broad aims and objectives. Performance Management cannot be regarded as a process involving only managers and their staff. As representatives of their electorate, councillors have a right and a duty to monitor local service delivery and to be involved in the review of both policy and performance.
- Councillors and managers in individual authorities do not, however, have a free hand in deciding their objectives and performance standards. These are increasingly determined by central government directly or by its auditing and inspection agencies which determine both the criteria by which they judge local authorities and the standards local authorities are required to achieve in relation to those criteria. It is increasingly unrealistic to suggest that performance can be freely determined and negotiated at the local level between councillors, managers and their staff.
- Judgements about the performance of local services and about their management are also increasingly made by the government and its agencies rather than by the local authority itself and the electorate. There is an increasing tendency for judgements about local 'success' and 'failure' to be publicly declaimed from London.
- The current concern for the quality of local democracy and for the need for local authorities to work in partnership with other agencies and organisations is leading to the involvement of a wider range of stakeholders in the process of determining, monitoring, reviewing and judging performance. These stakeholders include not just the customers of individual services but also citizens generally, local communities and other organisations involved in local public policy making and service delivery.

As a consequence of these conditions, it is necessary to attach a number of qualifications to any definition of Performance Management whilst at the same time recognising that, if Performance Management is to be a useful tool for local governance and services and service delivery, such a definition must be more wide-ranging than those provided above.

The definition does not attempt to specify the precise processes that are involved because it is considered more important to first define the general intent rather than express Performance Management as a set of techniques or procedures. Perhaps the major weakness of many attempts to implement Performance Management has been that it has been perceived only as a set of individual and often poorly interrelated techniques.

Definition of Performance Management

A set of interrelated and complementary processes concerned with:

- The development and sustenance of a culture and set of organisational values in which the ethical pursuit of improved performance is regarded as a legitimate and necessary part of the everyday workings of the organisation.
- The determination, communication and owning of the performance required of the organisation, and of the individuals within it, in terms of aims, objectives, standards and targets – in those areas where the requirement has not been pre-specified by the government and its agencies.
- The act of continuously managing performance, including the staff who are performing, once the performance requirement has been determined.
- The establishment of monitoring and review, evaluation or appraisal processes that focus in a balanced way on achieving conformance with planned performance and learning about how to improve performance.

An alternative way of considering Performance Management is to think of the fundamental organisational conditions that need to be achieved if a local authority is to successfully manage *all* the key aspects of its performance. Figure 1.1 expresses one way of viewing these conditions in a simplified way. The model uses two axes: one focuses on what is happening either inside or outside the organisation, the other represents the need for both control and flexibility. The four quadrants produced represent the four main conditions for managing performance in local government.

- **The need for stability and control** – the south-west quadrant (The well-regulated bureaucracy) represents the need to have a well-ordered organisation. This is achieved by developing control systems for regulating the way in which resources are used and accounted for and procedures and methods of working are developed and sustained in the organisation. Control and stability are also enhanced by good internal information systems that enable managers to know what is going on within the organisation. Typically there will also be a need for clear, formal systems of communication and co-ordination between the different parts of the organisation.

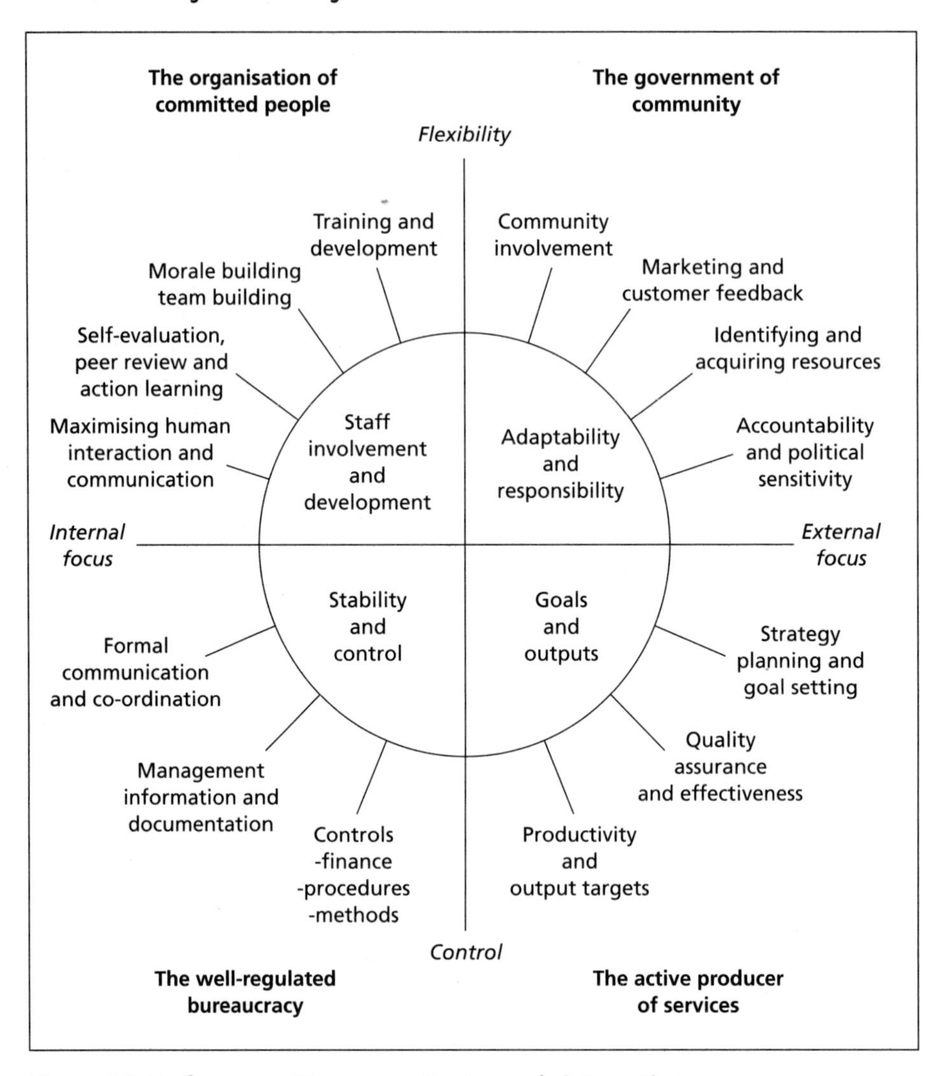

Figure 1.1 Performance Management – towards integration

- **Goals and outputs** – the south-east quadrant (The active producer of services) represents that part of organisational management that requires a focus on planning and monitoring what the organisation achieves for its community in terms of specified goals, outputs and service standards. This involves activities such as strategic and operational planning, developing procedures for assuring the quality and effectiveness of the outputs delivered as well as ensuring that the resources of the organisation are used productively and efficiently. The focus is on what is happening externally – that is, the services that are delivered to the community – and also on control, in the sense of ensuring that the planned services are actually delivered.

- **Staff development and involvement** – sustaining a focus on goals and outputs cannot be achieved without actively involving the staff of the organisation. Not only do staff need to be committed to the current goals and outputs, they also need to be motivated to respond to the inevitable need to change the organisation's goals from time to time and to continuously adapt and improve performance. The north-west quadrant therefore focuses on change and flexibility of staff within the organisation and is labelled 'The organisation of committed people.' The management activities in this quadrant include systems for self and peer evaluation, creating opportunities for active learning, formal and informal training and development programmes as well as ensuring that staff can interact and communicate appropriately.
- **Adaptability and responsiveness** – the north-east quadrant (The government of community) represents the requirement for all local authorities to have the capacity to work with their communities and with other institutions of government and public service. They also have to be able to adapt and respond to the demands and expectations of their external environment – a capacity that lies at the heart of the concept of community governance. The managerial implications of this aspect of management are that a local authority should have the competence to undertake marketing and to obtain feedback from customers and citizens, that it should also be accountable to, and sensitive of, the changing requirements and expectations of the local political process, and that it should work in partnership with other organisations. Increasingly local authorities also have to be more creative and flexible in the way they acquire and use resources on behalf of and with their communities – a requirement which in some cases leads to more direct involvement of the community in designing and delivering services.

This diagrammatic representation of performance management helps to illustrate two important issues. First, that the four conditions of management are in tension with each other. Good management requires not just a focus on what is happening inside the authority but also what is happening outside. Both are fundamentally important and there needs to be a balance between the two. Equally, there needs to be a balance between achieving control, and the consequential tendency to keep affairs stable, while at the same time ensuring that the organisation can change and be flexible. One without the other creates an unbalanced form of management. The second issue illustrated by this analysis is that a good model of performance management is one in which there is an appropriate focus on all four quadrants. Without sufficient internal control the organisation is liable to become unstable; without planning the outputs and outcomes expected of the organisation it is less likely to produce efficient and effective services; without committed and developing staff it will be unable to sustain its achievement of goals; and without the capacity to adapt and respond to its environment it is increasingly likely to become perceived as irrelevant and subject to increasing criticism. Achieving a balanced focus on all four aspects of management is not easy and requires constant review and adjustment of the systems, procedures and processes in each quadrant.

Figure 1.1 may also be interpreted historically as depicting how the primary focus of management has shifted in recent years. It may be argued that the primary focus of many traditional local authorities was on achieving stability and control. Subsequently the main effect of the introduction of Performance Management, coupled with the public sector reforms of the 1980s and early 1990s, was to shift the focus onto the achievement of specified goals and outputs and, to a lesser extent, the introduction of more systems and procedures concerned with motivating, involving and developing staff. Performance Management, in its different manifestations, can be seen to have had an influence on all three of these aspects of management. Where it has had less impact, at least until now, is in the fourth quadrant, the government of the community, where the many developments that have occurred in local government have been achieved independently of the management systems and approaches associated with Performance Management. It may be argued that the current government's agenda for modernising local government is, at least in part, an attempt to use some of the principles and techniques of Performance Management in the pursuit of better community governance.

The processes and systems for managing performance

Performance Management, now that it has been implemented either wholly or partly by many local authorities, tends to consist of a common set of processes and systems that may be regarded as representing a 'model' approach. They can be described as follows and are summarised diagrammatically in Figure 1.2.

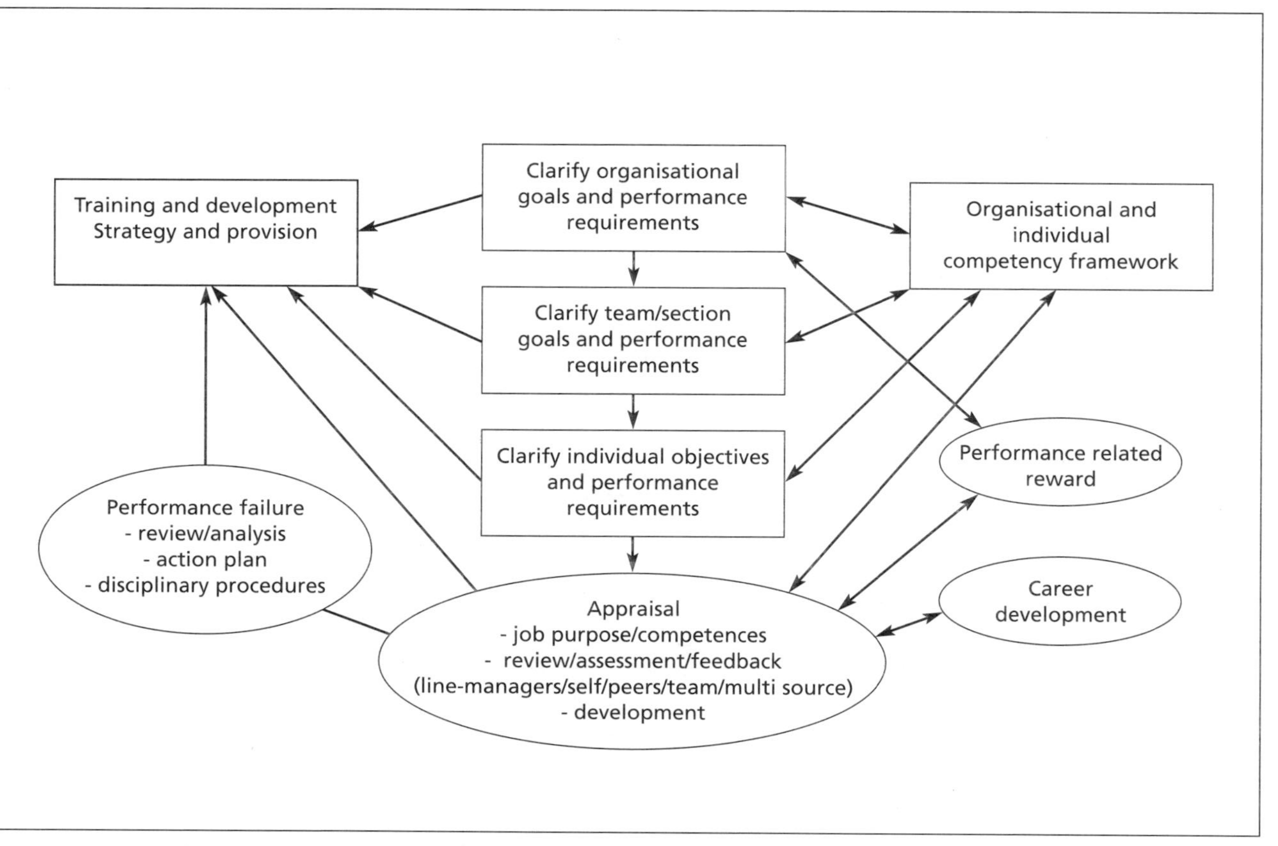

Figure 1.2 A model for managing organisational and individual performance

- Specifying and stating the overall mission, vision, purpose and values of the local authority.
- Specifying, clarifying and agreeing the aims and objectives of the authority by means of an integrated set of planning processes that may include: community planning; corporate planning; policy led budget planning; service development planning; and business planning.
- Communicating and reinforcing, in a variety of ways, the mission, vision, values, goals, aims and objectives to all councillors, staff, customers, citizens and partner organisations.
- Identifying and developing the organisational competencies, capabilities and capacities that are required to achieve the specified mission, aims and objectives.
- Cascading the aims and objectives down through each tier of the organisation so that they can be ultimately related to the responsibilities and performance of each individual member of staff.
- Monitoring and reviewing organisational performance by developing information systems and review procedures at suitable levels in the organisation that directly and appropriately involve councillors, managers, staff, service users, citizens and partner organisations.
- Consistently and regularly appraising, reviewing and developing the performance of individuals (and in some cases, teams) and planning their career progression and development.
- Developing a strategy for organisational and individual performance development and improvement.
- Developing and implementing strategies for appropriately rewarding and recognising individual and team performance.
- Developing a strategy and the competencies required to deal with 'performance failure' – whether that be organisational or individual.

While not all these processes will be found in every local authority that claims to have implemented Performance Management, they do represent a 'model' to which many local authorities appear to aspire. Examples of some of the different ways in which local authorities have attempted to develop this model are explored in Chapters 6 and 7.

The growth of Performance Management

Local authorities have responded to the external pressures and ideas surrounding them by introducing a variety of systems that are most frequently described as 'Performance Management' but which sometimes are given alternative labels. The 1991 Recruitment and Retention survey carried out by the Local Government Management Board (LGMB) revealed that 35 per cent of responding local authorities claimed to be operating Performance Management and 23 per cent had plans to introduce it (LGMB, 1993). A later LGMB survey conducted in 1993 showed that 44 per cent of the 279 authorities responding claimed to have implemented some explicit form of Performance Management and a further 14 per cent were planning to implement a scheme of some kind. Less than 1 per cent had withdrawn after implementing a scheme and only 7 per cent had explicitly decided not to pursue Performance Management (LGMB, 1993). Ignoring for the moment the question of exactly how each authority chose to define Performance Management, it is nonetheless clear that it has had a significant impact on local government and even those councils which did not claim to have a 'scheme' were likely in practice to have implemented at least some elements of Performance Management. Some authorities have decided, for various reasons, to avoid using the term 'performance' as a label for any of their management processes. For example, Oxfordshire County Council has a scheme for managing individual performance which many authorities would refer to as 'performance appraisal' or 'individual performance review', but in Oxfordshire neither of these terms were used because they were felt to imply an approach which was unsympathetic to Oxfordshire's particular reasons for introducing the scheme. Other local authorities, such as the London Borough of Brent, prefer to use variations on the theme of 'quality' as a label for their management processes.

Is Performance Management a distinctive management approach?

Different writers describe and define Performance Management in different ways. In some cases, as has been demonstrated in the Nutley and Osborne approach, the definition is narrow, relating only to processes for measuring and reviewing organisational performance. In other cases, such as the author's own definition and description provided above, Performance Management is represented in a wider and more all-embracing way. Local authorities also use the term differently, there being four broad categories of usage. In some authorities the term appears to be used in a very general, almost symbolic way to represent the general style or approach of the authority and without being related to any specific systems or processes. In other authorities it is used specifically in relation to a set of procedures and techniques designed to ensure the proper management of organisational performance. The third usage is in relation only to those systems and procedures for managing the performance of individual employees and the fourth category embraces the processes and techniques for managing, in an integrated way, both organisational and individual performance.

Given the breadth and variety of definitions the question arises as to whether 'Performance Management' is really a distinctive body of management concepts and techniques or whether it is just a convenient umbrella label given to a number of approaches that may appear similar but do not, in fact, have any fundamental coherence or relationship.

Throughout this chapter the term 'Performance Management' has been capitalised, thereby suggesting that it is a singular and identifiable object. But it may be argued that it would be better presented in the lower case, thereby reflecting that it is simply a collection of different concepts and techniques that have become associated with the general need to improve the performance of organisations. By changing this emphasis in this way it may be possible to thereby reduce the need for 'Performance Management' to be seen as an industry in its own right requiring the use of experts to instruct local authority councillors, managers and staff in how to do what they themselves must be expert at – managing their own performance in serving their local communities! It may be more relevant and meaningful to refer to 'the management of performance' or 'managing for performance' than to 'Performance Management'. In the following chapters 'Performance Management' will become 'performance management'.

2

The changing performance requirement

Introduction

The purpose of this chapter is to outline the main legislative changes that have influenced the way in which the concept of performance, and the way in which it is managed, have become defined, and to identify the ways in which local government has responded to these changes.

In Chapter 1 it was suggested that performance management should be thought of as more than a specific management system or set of techniques. It may be seen as the product of a number of contextual pressures and expectations. As a broad concept applied to public service management it is based on and is influenced by a particular set of political and societal values, ethics and assumptions that have been translated into legislative requirements by successive governments. These requirements determine both the concept itself and the way it is interpreted and implemented in the public sector. It has also been shaped and influenced by a set of management concepts and practices many of which have been developed in the private sector. These concepts and practices are both shaped by, and in turn, influence the political, economic and ethical context in which they are developed.

The main themes of the government's legislative programme

Local authorities have been subject to a programme of reforms, applied by successive governments since the early 1980s, that have required them to reconsider not just **how** performance should best be managed but also **what** performance is required of them and **by whom** local services should be provided. They have also been forced to reconsider **who** should set their performance standards and make judgements about their performance. While the dominant declared objective of the reforms of the Thatcher and Major governments was the pursuit of greater economy, efficiency and effectiveness, there were also wider objectives that included the redefinition of the role of local government – a more fundamental change which sought to alter the basis of the relationship between local authorities and their citizens and between central and local government.

The legislative programme arose from an analysis of local government that was highly critical of both political and managerial decision making and that was, itself, part of a much broader programme of reform of the public sector. This included an even more radical transformation of the structure and management of the NHS, the transfer of some central government functions from departments to newly created agencies, the opening up of government functions to market testing, and the transfer of central and local government functions to 'quangos' such as Training and Enterprise Councils and Hospital Trusts. The wellspring for many of these reforms was a number of think-tanks such as the Institute of Economic Affairs and the Adam Smith Institute which lay outside the usual policy formulation processes in the government's own departments and on which the government became increasingly reliant, thereby effectively 'contracting out' much of the policy formulation process. The reform programme also involved the creation of new information and control systems to enable Ministers to achieve tighter control over their departments, of which the first and perhaps best known was the Financial Management Initiative (FMI) introduced by Michael Heseltine in the mid 1980s when Secretary of State for the Environment.

The 1980s and 1990s have been characterised by a constant flow of legislation, Ministerial directives and accompanying regulations directed at local authorities. Underlying the legislation have been a number of themes that have had both a direct and indirect impact on the way in which performance management has been introduced and developed in local government. These themes (which are discussed in more detail below) are as follows:

- accountability
- the explosion of audit and inspection
- customer choice
- competition and contractualisation
- the centralisation and control of government
- the Citizens Charter

- reorganisation
- employment and trade union legislation
- ethics and standards in public life.

Accountability

The perceived lack of accountability of local government has been a continuing and basic theme of public sector reform. From early requirements to publish annual reports, through the ill-fated attempt to increase public accountability by means of the poll tax, to the publication of performance indicators as part of the Citizens Charter, the theme of accountability is constant and dominant. It is perhaps best represented by the setting up of the Widdicombe Committee, its report in 1986 and the subsequent legislation in 1989 which created numerous regulations concerning such matters as: twin-tracking (i.e. staff in one authority acting as councillors in another); the appointment of political advisers; proportionality of political party representation on committees; the specification of key officer roles – including that of a monitoring officer; and procedures for the dismissal of chief executives.

The more extensive use of contracts, both within local authorities and between them and private and voluntary sector providers of service was also a central part of the accountability drive, with formal, written contracts seen as better mechanisms for achieving accountability than traditional forms of decision making. The principle of contracting was also extended to individual employees with top managers being made accountable by means of time-limited performance contracts.

Accountability is a simple concept but the mechanisms for achieving it tend to be complex and multiple. As a consequence it is not surprising that the pursuit of accountability took several forms.

- Making local government more accountable to central government – especially for its use of centrally provided resources and for the delivery of nationally determined policies and standards.
- Making each local authority more accountable to its citizens, local taxpayers and communities by recognising that accountability through the ballot box was insufficient, particularly in view of the relatively low turnout at local elections compared to many other European democracies.
- Making each local authority service more accountable to its users. This was in practice the main driving force behind the Citizens Charter and the provisions for opting out by schools and council house tenants.

- Making managers in local authorities more directly accountable to their councillors. Privately, and sometimes publicly, councillors of all political persuasions had been critical of the failure of professionally dominated departments to adequately respond to legitimate political objectives. The debate about 'member-officer relations' during the 1980s not infrequently centred around the issue of whether a local authority was really run by its councillors or its officers. Councillors looked for ways of making their professionals and managers more accountable and drew on models of performance management provided by government and the private sector in order to achieve their objective.
- Making the base of the employee hierarchy more accountable to the apex. If some officers were unsure whether they really wanted the discipline of being held individually accountable to their councillors they nonetheless quickly realised that if they were to be held so accountable then they needed to supplement the historical bureaucratic and professional forms of accountability with new managerial forms. Foremost amongst these was the concept of performance contracts and appraisals for individuals and the introduction of more performance-oriented service and business planning procedures.

The extent of accountability reforms and the number of resulting mechanisms for achieving it would appear to make local government highly accountable. There remain, however, a number of unresolved questions which cast doubt on whether this is so.

- Is each form of accountability appropriate and effective?
- Do the multiple forms of accountability create a confusing rather than a clear picture for the individual citizen when deciding how to hold the local authority to account?
- Do the different forms of accountability operate in a consistent way or do they create avoidable conflicts and tensions?
- To whom is accountability strongest? Many of the reforms have been intended to make local government more accountable to central government rather than to local citizens.
- Does the existence of multiple accountability requirements have a negative impact on the development of a culture of internal accountability, self-regulation and performance improvement?

The explosion of audit and inspection

The title of this section has, in an amended form, been borrowed from Michael Power's pamphlet, 'The Audit Explosion' (Power, 1994). In this he develops eight arguments to demonstrate that there has been a qualitative as well as a quantitative shift in the role of audit – producing a situation where 'many more individuals and organisations are coming to think of themselves as subject to audit.' His arguments are of importance to the way that performance management has and will be developed and the most important is that audit needs to be understood as an 'idea' and not just as a set of technical and operational procedures.

> *Audit has become central to ways of talking about administrative control. The extension of auditing into different settings... is more than a natural and self-evidently technical response to problems of government and accountability. It has much to do with articulating values, with rationalising and reinforcing images of public control. The audit explosion is the explosion of an idea that is internal to the ways in which practitioners and policy makers make sense of what they are doing. (Power, 1994)*

Power also argues that the spread of audits 'corresponds to a fundamental shift in patterns of government in advanced industrial societies' which results from a concern that traditional control structures are increasingly unable to cope with the risks produced by an advanced industrial society, most obviously in areas such as medicine and the environment. Audit has become the means of trying to reconcile two contradictory forces:

> *... on the one hand the need to extend a traditional hierarchical command conception of control in order to maintain existing structures of authority; on the other the need to cope with the failure of this type of control, as it generates risks that are increasingly hard to specify and control. (Power, 1994)*

There has, without any doubt, been a significant increase in the use of both external and internal audit and inspection. In addition to the familiar notion of financial audits, there are now also value for money audits, management audits, data audits, environmental audits, quality audits, medical audits and probably many others. The creation of the Audit Commission and the National Audit Office in the early 1980s consolidated the auditing arrangements for local and central government and the NHS, establishing two powerful institutions with the duty and power to scrutinise the economy, efficiency and effectiveness of public expenditure and provision. In local government the powers of auditors were extended to include reporting on value for money, writing an annual management letter and, as required by the Audit Commission, carrying out in-depth analyses of particular services with the Commission itself conducting an extensive programme of national studies. The role of the Audit Commission has continued to expand and now includes responsibilities not only in relation to financial and value for money auditing but also to inspection and the determination of performance indicators. Its role will increase yet further with the introduction of a Best Value regime (see Chapter 3).

The power of the inspection agencies has also increased considerably, most notably the unprecedented dominance of OFSTED not only with regard to the inspection of schools but also the determination of standards and the development of education policy. The Social Service Inspectorate has also in recent years considerably extended the range and influence of its activities. Perhaps the clearest indication that we have become what has been referred to as 'an audit society' is that external audit and inspection agencies are now being combined – as evidenced by the joint reviews of Social Services Departments undertaken by the Audit Commission and the Social Services Inspectorate.

The relevance of the audit explosion for performance management is that it is being developed in circumstances which are mutually contradictory. While performance management aims to increase the capacity of councillors and managers to determine and manage the performance of their own affairs it is being applied in an environment where both the definition of performance and the operational processes for achieving that performance are being increasingly determined not just by central government but by wholly or partly autonomous audit and inspection agencies. Rather than encouraging an approach of self-reliance, responsibility and creativity they are likely to produce a culture of compliance and conformance – with worrying consequences. Performing becomes mere conforming. In a climate of tight control, service providers will tend to conform to the requirement and expectations of the auditors and inspectors – or will seek to give the impression of so doing. The former can create genuine benefits if the inspectors and auditors use sound concepts and methodologies. But they may not and definitions and standards of performance may become limited by their assumptions, interests and expertise.

It is not surprising that some of the approaches to performance management which have emerged in local government reflect the climate of increased control and conformance, producing what Metcalfe and Richards (1987) referred to as an 'impoverished' form of management. It is an approach which has sometimes led to managing performance being reduced to just measuring performance and its use as a rather blunt instrument of control.

Customer choice

Choice is an extension of the principle of accountability. While accountability has often focused on the provision of an 'account', be it in the form of an annual report, a set of performance indicators or a service or 'citizens' contract, the ability of both customers and citizens to hold a local authority to account has been limited to mechanisms such as voting in elections, participating directly in the political process and complaining. The legislative provision of choice, particularly the choice provided to traditional customers such as council house tenants and the parents of school children to 'opt out' of local authority provision, represents a fundamental shift in the balance of power from the local authority to the customer. Local authorities, if they wish to remain service providers, have to perform in a way that is most likely to result in the retention of their customers whilst at the same time providing them with the performance information which allows their customers to make judgements about that performance. But it is the existence of choice, rather than the provision of an account, which has stimulated a fundamental reappraisal of services.

Competition and contractualisation

The impact of increased competition and the use of contracts on the way performance management has developed has been considerable and may be summarised as follows.

- Compulsory Competitive Tendering (CCT) forced local authorities, often for the first time, to develop clear specifications and performance criteria for their services.
- Because authorities found it difficult to determine appropriate quality criteria, and because of the rules relating to the evaluation and acceptance of tenders, CCT resulted in a primary focus on cost and volume performance criteria.
- CCT created the need for new financial and performance management systems, particularly in Direct Service Organisations (DSOs), which led to the development of innovative information systems and management practices. The extent to which these innovations have been transferred to those parts of local authorities not subject to CCT has, however, been variable.
- CCT has created tensions within local authorities where services are provided by DSOs. Having to operate within a 'bottom line' performance indicator of a specified rate of return on capital employed, DLO managers were forced to question the cost and quality of the support services they received from their authority.
- The general climate of increased competition created a sharper focus on performance issues in all local authority departments. It also, as was intended, created a climate of uncertainty which was new to local government.

- The use of performance-based contracts as a basis for service provision became widespread. Contracts were used not only with external contractors but also with voluntary agencies, that had formerly received grants-in-aid, and other partner organisations. Contracts, in the form of service or management agreements, also became the basis for the provision of services within authorities.
- Contracting was also applied to individual employees, with senior managers and some other employees having time-limited, performance-based contracts.
- The compulsory use of competition within the CCT regime has prevented local authorities from undertaking a strategic review of the best method of service delivery for those services subject to it. The presumption in favour of the private sector and the use of arms-length methods of contracting has been a limiting factor in the pursuit of improved performance.

The above points are not intended to be a full evaluation of CCT and the consequential increased use of contracts. That has been done elsewhere (see for example Walsh and Davies, 1993). They are intended to illustrate the mix of benefits and problems that resulted from this increased use. It is unlikely that performance management would have developed as fast or as extensively without CCT, but equally it is likely that it would have developed in a different way with more emphasis on quality and a greater recognition that good performance results from a positive relationship between client and contractor.

The centralisation and control of government

A strong tendency of both the Thatcher and Major governments was to centralise and extend government control over increasing areas of national life – in direct contradiction to the declared message of reducing the role of government and rolling back the frontiers of the welfare state. In practice, ministers accumulated power within an increasingly overburdened central state while emasculating the local state. As Jenkins (1997) has illustrated, much of this centralisation took place, not as many would expect during the Thatcher government, but during the subsequent Major governments.

> *Thatcher's centralisation gathered pace...(under Major)....it extended further into the running of the NHS, the new police authorities, housing, the railways, the schools and universities and the administration of justice. The abandonment of the poll tax in favour of the council tax led to a decrease rather than an increase in local authority discretion. (Jenkins, 1997)*

Jenkins also argues that this centralisation occurred despite the increased public rhetoric of partnership, the improved relations between central government and the leaders of the local government associations and the agreement of a set of principles for governing the relationship between central and local government. The reality was very different with the removal from local authorities of responsibility for further education, sixth-form colleges and the police, the extension of CCT to white-collar services and the further encouragement of opting-out by schools. In addition, the increased severity of both the grant settlements and financial capping arrangement brought local authority expenditure decisions increasingly under direct central control by the mid 1990s.

The sheer extent of control cannot be underestimated. An article by one well-known commentator on local government finance was headlined 'Stalin would have been impressed. Even he could not have established such detailed control over local programmes as Whitehall has achieved' and contained the assertion that:

> *No other country makes anything like the effort the British do to fine tune a service-by-service spending need measurement for each local authority in the land.... Perhaps it was inevitable Mrs T's decentralising, liberalising government could have come up with such effective tools of democratic centralism. (Travers, 1996)*

The effect of this centralism with respect to performance management was much the same as that created by the audit explosion. While the government was requiring local authorities to take greater responsibility for improving their performance, it was at the same time reducing their real responsibility for their own actions by removing services, reducing local discretion and increasing its own powers.

The Citizens Charter

While it is clear that the government's intention in introducing the Citizens Charter was to improve the performance of public service organisations it is less clear what has really been achieved. The proposals contained in the 1991 Citizens Charter White Paper were based on six principles which public service organisations were required to follow.

- To publish the standards and targets they set themselves and the performance they achieved against those standards and targets.
- To consult with the users of their services in setting standards.
- To give information in plain language about the range of services available.

- To provide a courteous and efficient customer service.
- To maintain a responsive complaints service, with some means for independent review.
- To ensure that their performance is validated independently and that they have a clear commitment to value for money.

The Citizens Charter was just one element in an enormous drive towards the introduction of charters throughout the public sector. Charters were created for parents, patients, tenants, and the users of all the privatised utilities. Most charters were intended to contain a mixture of rights to know and rights to choose but little real attention was given to how the latter right was to be achieved.

The two most important consequences for local authorities were the requirement to measure and publish their performance against a set of performance indicators and the introduction of the Citizens Charter Marks. The subsequent 1992 Local Government Act required the Audit Commission to determine a set of performance indicators for all local government services. All local authorities were then required to record their own performance against the specified indicators, to publish details in local newspapers and to provide the information to the Audit Commission – which was required to publish the results nationally. The requirement was groundbreaking. No other democratic government had attempted such a high degree of control in its detailed prescription of the way in which the performance of local government was to be defined and measured. The response was, at times, antagonistic, indignant or derisive. For example:

> *It is a 1960s accountancy approach that focuses on statistics, which gives answers to strange questions, culminating in the thickest stew of indigestible statistics ever produced that will then be squeezed into local newspapers between ironing boards and 1972 Ford Escorts. (Keenan, 1994)*

But in many cases it also prompted a fundamental review of the shortcomings of local authority current practices.

> *At the present time the Council has no systematic long term process to ensure the continuing relevance of services, no statement of assumptions underlying service standards, nor any formal investigation of alternative methods of providing individual service activities. (1993 report to the Performance Review Committee of a District Council)*

A more detailed analysis of the Citizens Charter performance indicators is contained in Chapter 5 and it is therefore sufficient to state here that this requirement, coupled with other legislative requirements for particular services such as housing, schools and colleges, to publish their performance against prescribed indicators, has resulted in an enormous volume of comparative data about local authorities' performance and, consequentially, much more political, professional and media analysis of the performance of local authorities. It has also resulted in a continuing debate about the relevance and reliability of many of the indicators. Whether such indicators are used by citizens is also open to debate but appears to be doubtful. They are clearly used within local authorities but the extent and type of use appears to vary significantly.

The most important issue in judging the effect of the indicators is whether they have resulted in an improvement in performance, at least with respect to the limited criteria of performance that they measure. The Audit Commission's annual comparative data publications suggest that there has been improvement amongst the worst performing authorities on some of the indicators, but there is much less evidence of improvement amongst average and better performing authorities (Vevers, 1998). Of more concern is the possibility that recorded improvements may be cosmetic rather than real, with local authorities having learned to 'play the game'.

The other significant aspect of the Citizens Charter in relation to local authority performance management was the introduction of Charter Marks which were launched in 1992 and presented as a personal initiative of the Prime Minister. Intended to be a form of quality assurance they operated in an increasingly crowded field of 'kite-marks', 'badges', competitive awards and certification processes. The Charter Mark process does not compare favourably with some other forms of quality assurance and certification such as the British Quality Foundation and the British Standards Institute, its main weakness being the lack of precise standards of assessment used in relation to the nine broadly specified performance criteria. Criticisms have also been made of the minimal amount of training given to the assessors and their lack of prior experience.

But whatever their validity, and despite being initially opposed by organisations such as the Trades Union Congress, the Charter Marks have proved to be very popular, especially amongst local authorities which have been particularly successful in winning them. In the first year, 36 Citizens Charter Marks were awarded of which local authorities won 10 (28 per cent) – having submitted only 16 per cent of the applications. In 1995 (by which time the government had discretely removed the word 'citizens' from the title) local authorities submitted 232 applications, second only to health authorities in number. Of these, 84 local authorities won Charter Marks, a success rate of 36 per cent and they accounted for approximately one third of the 223 winners.

Whether they are in any sense a guarantee of good service is open to considerable doubt and they may be of little perceived relevance to the public generally. Perhaps their most important role is in massaging the battered egos of public service providers and providing them with some, albeit limited, sense of success.

Reorganisation

In the context of performance management, the main impact of the local government reorganisations during the 1990s was to stimulate a considerable amount of creative thinking not just in the new unitary authorities but also in those counties and districts in England which were eager to achieve unitary status. Although there was a tendency to concentrate on organisational structures there was also evidence of an intention to develop new forms of relationships with, and responsiveness to, service users, citizens and communities. In some cases this was extended to reconsideration of styles of management and methods of service delivery. The requirement placed on unitary authorities in Wales to produce Service Development Plans, and the requirement in Scotland to produce Schemes of Delegation, had an added impact in forcing the new authorities to develop new ideas for managing and delivering their services.

Employment and trade union legislation

The reduction in the legal powers of trade unions in the 1980s altered the balance of power between employees and employers. Some local authorities took advantage of this shift by reducing the role and status of the unions, by removing restrictive practices, by introducing more open-ended contracts of employment and by introducing management systems that had previously been opposed by the unions.

Other local authorities maintained the role and status of trade unions and also sought to maintain traditional employment conditions in pursuit of their aim of being a model employer. However, economic conditions and the introduction of competition, rather than legislation, have had the greatest impact on the conditions and circumstances of employment in local government during the 1990s, resulting in a marked shift in assumptions and practices – as well as in the number of people employed.

The election of a Labour government in 1997 was seen by some as a signal for a renewed role for trade unions and the introduction of better legal protection for employees, but the government has, after one year, shown little indication of its willingness to make any significant changes.

Ethics and standards in public life

The rising concern about ethical standards in corporate governance has been evident in both the private and public sectors. In the private sector, the Committee on the Financial Aspects of Corporate Governance (The Cadbury Committee, 1992) produced a code of best practice which, although much criticised, has been subsequently revised and remains in operation. One central feature of the code, the establishment of Audit Committees, has on several occasions been proposed as relevant to local government. For the public sector, the Committee on Standards in Public Life (The Nolan Committee), which was set up in the wake of continuing concern about 'sleaze', has produced several reports which, apart from their specific recommendations and proposals, ascribe fundamental importance to ensuring that all decision-making structures, roles and systems are based on a strong positive ethical basis. In its first report, the Committee set out 'Seven Principles of Public Life': selflessness, integrity, objectivity, accountability, openness, honesty and leadership.

Local government already has its own standards and codes of conduct, for example the Code of Conduct for Local Government Employees (Association of Metropolitan Authorities *et al.*) which explicitly covers relationships with contractors and potential contractors. The main political parties also have their own codes and rules – for example the Labour Party's Rules for Local Government Labour Groups (Labour Party, 1996) require all Labour councillors 'to uphold the highest standards of probity and integrity' and to go beyond the statutory requirements for registering and declaring their interests.

The Labour government, concerned that Labour controlled councils are a very visible manifestation of the Labour Party in power, has repeatedly expressed its concern. The Prime Minister has argued that 'the way local government currently operates is inefficient and opaque' and has also stated that:

> *Councillors and officials who are incompetent or corrupt not only undermine their leadership credentials but sully the reputation of local government as a whole. We cannot and will not tolerate corruption and malpractice. (Blair, 1998)*

In the press some critics have been more trenchant. Freedland, for example, asserts that 'a viscous river of sleaze trickles along the corridors of local government', and this 'reflects the poverty of our local democracy'. He goes on to assert that local government must:

> *...shed the myth of our own incorruptibility. We have long assumed corruption to be a far away malady – endemic in Italy or Latin America, but hardly a worry here. (Freedland, 1998)*

But notions of corruption and unethical behaviour are not always clear-cut and what such statements fail to acknowledge is that the styles of government and management that are increasingly required and expected of local authorities are themselves a major contributor to creating a new 'grey area' of ethical uncertainty. Partnership, joint working, gaining 'leverage', indeed much of the substance of the 'new public management', all create circumstances where traditional definitions of corruption can be easily and clearly applied. In the area of external contracting, the numerous benefits of moving away from the rigid bureaucracy of the CCT legislation to more flexible models of relational contracting also have to be balanced against the ethical uncertainties that will result from their use. The closer the relationship between client and contractor the greater the possibilities for corruption. The rhetoric of 'partnership' is also a source of ethical uncertainty which may be unacknowledged. The Department of the Environment, Transport and the Regions has recently stated that a key feature of Best Value will be effective partnership which:

> *...requires a different approach, which reflects the characteristics of the service in question and the preferences of the private and voluntary sectors, as well as service users. (DETR, 1998a)*

It may be argued that 'responding to the preferences of the private and voluntary sectors' in a way which is publicly accountable and transparent will require new rules for ensuring accountability and for determining what is and is not ethically defensible behaviour.

The present government's proposals for creating a Standards Board and for Standards Committees to be set up in each local authority (DETR, 1998b) may go some way to ensuring that there is a continuing debate about how councillors and officers should be permitted to behave while pursuing current concepts of good governance and management.

The local government response

Faced with the reforming zeal of the newly elected government and influenced by an awareness of what is regarded as good management practice in the private sector and by the advice and influence of bodies such as the Audit Commission, local authorities began to look at new ways of managing their affairs. But the pressure to change was not just external. Local authority councillors were also increasingly critical of the failings of their own organisations and were looking for ways in which their managers could be made more accountable to them and the efficiency and quality of the services they provided improved. The critique of the public sector may have been led by the Thatcher government but it found a resonance in local politicians of all political parties. The solutions advocated by each of the main parties may have differed in their precise shape but the underlying critique found fertile ground across the political spectrum.

Performance management was one of the dominant solutions. Although initially introduced in Conservative controlled authorities such as Cambridgeshire, Bexley and Arun, it soon spread widely. By the late 1980s it was no longer an approach which could be exclusively associated either with the government or with Conservative local authorities.

However, not all authorities introduced performance management in the same way or for the same reasons. Informal research carried out by the author during the 1980s and early 1990s suggested that local authorities were using performance management in response to different pressures and for different purposes. The precise mix of pressures and objectives gave rise to approaches to performance management which differed in both substance and style. These will be discussed in Chapter 6.

Conclusion

Legislative reforms have combined with local political aspirations and managerial concepts to produce a new set of managerial approaches, sometimes labelled the 'New Public Management', of which performance management is, in most respects, the most characteristic and important. But the new management, while creating solutions also raises questions. Among the questions raised by this chapter are the following.

- How can a new ethos and ethic be constructed which combines the special and essential characteristics of public service with the new approaches to management intended to improve its performance?
- How can individual initiative and responsibility amongst both officers and councillors be released and rewarded while at the same time strengthening collective accountability, security and responsibility?
- How can the relationship with service users and citizens be transformed from one of paternalistic hierarchy to one in which they are active participants?

- How can competition be balanced with co-operation, thereby releasing its positive and creative, rather than its destructive and conflictive power?
- How can the professional and technical skills and competencies of public servants be mobilised without succumbing to the tyranny of the professional?

3

Best Value

'Re-election in recognition of performance is the ultimate reward in a democratic society.' (DETR, 1998a, para 6.11)

Introduction

The previous chapter focused primarily on the changes introduced by successive Conservative governments, some of which appear to have been accepted by the Labour government elected in May 1997. But one of those changes – Compulsory Competitive tendering (CCT) – was not accepted and this chapter explores the new government's proposed alternative – Best Value. Best Value is only one of many new policy and legislative initiatives directed at local authorities but, in the context of performance management, it is the most important for the following reasons.

- It is fundamental to the future management of all of local government. It lays down a comprehensive framework for both managing and holding local authorities to account and, as the Prime Minister has stated (Blair, 1998), it is not just an alternative to CCT – it has more wide-ranging objectives and implications.
- It is explicitly based on the principles of performance management. The Department of the Environment, Transport and the Regions (DETR) describes the government's basic process for achieving Best Value as a 'Performance Management Framework.' (DETR, 1998a)

The perception of CCT

The intention to replace CCT with a Best Value regime emerged from three competing concerns. First, there was sufficient evidence that CCT had been only partially successful in making the production of local services more economical and efficient, particularly when the transactional costs associated with it are taken into account (see for example: Walsh (1991) and Walsh and Davies (1993)). Second, there were widespread and strong objections based on an analysis that it was overly rigid, prevented initiatives, was ideologically biased in favour of the private sector, and was based on a model of contractual relationships that was no longer considered to be good practice. Other evidence, such as its disproportionately adverse effect on lower paid workers and, in particular, females (see for example: Centre for Public Services, 1995) presented important issues for the new Labour government. The third concern is not documented explicitly but it is apparent that some members of the government took the view that, even if CCT had not been as successful as previous governments had hoped and claimed, it was nonetheless a key form of discipline and control over local councils. Given that the primary aim of the new government was to contain public spending, there was a concern that any proposal to abolish CCT would be taken as a signal that councils were free to return to earlier practices and to spend more freely. Therefore, despite agreeing with local government about the failings of CCT, the government did not wish to rush ahead with its abolition until it was certain that it had a robust and workable alternative in place.

The policy background

The origins of Best Value may be traced back to the Labour Party's 1995 policy statement on local government, 'Renewing Democracy, Rebuilding Communities' (Labour Party, 1995), in which reference was made to the concept of a 'local performance programme.' This reference was itself a development of the concept of 'annual community plans' contained in an earlier, consultative version of the statement (Rogers, 1998). The local performance programme was presented as part of 'a better approach' than CCT.

> *We propose to introduce a new system designed to secure the very best quality services and value for money with pressure for continuous improvements. We believe the best guarantee is to involve local people in the whole process of setting targets, achieving standards and monitoring costs. Each year, every council would be required to spell out to local people its quality and cost targets for each service for the forthcoming year and how it had performed against its existing targets. Local people would then have redress against failure to meet those targets. Annual publication by the Audit Commission of indicators of performance for every council would make it easy for local people, councillors and staff to judge the performance of their council against that of comparable councils and so bring about further pressure for improvements. This process would be based on a local performance programme which would be formulated by each council in consultation with local people generally and with users of specific services. It would set out objectives, priorities and performance targets for each service and the cost implications for local people, local businesses and voluntary organisations. It would be updated each year and include targets for year-on-year improvements. In addition, central government grant to local councils could include an incentive for year on year improvements in standards. (Labour Party, 1995)*

Taken alone, the proposal for performance programmes can be seen as just an extension of the existing Citizens Charter performance indicator regime with more emphasis on objective and target setting and consultation. But it was linked to other proposals in a way that indicated that it was meant to be much more than that. These proposals were: developing more national standards to be monitored by the Audit Commission; strengthening of the powers and practices of the District Audit Service to deal with financial scandals; 'refocusing' the Audit Commission into a 'standards inspectorate' and extending its powers to include the determination of whether local services were 'failing or costing more than could be justified.' (Labour Party, 1995). In such an event it was proposed that the Commission would have the power to require the council to produce and implement an improvement plan, to set up an advisory team to help the council, and to check on both progress and outcome of the plan. Finally, there was a proposal for the Secretary of State to be given the power to appoint management teams to take over services until they were improved.

Several themes emerge from this first attempt to formulate what eventually became Best Value:

- the reliance on and extension of powers of the Audit Commission;
- the focus on the concept of continuous improvement;
- the reliance on the basic performance management concepts of objective and target setting and monitoring;
- the importance attached to local consultation;
- the concern for 'failing' councils and services;
- the general increase in the external control of local government by central government and its auditing and inspecting agencies – a theme which lies oddly with other government pronouncements about the need for partnership and declarations of the importance of local self-government.

The new government's first programme of legislation did not refer to the abolition of CCT. Given a shortage of parliamentary time, the repeal of CCT, which required primary legislation, did not achieve sufficient priority and, perhaps more importantly – despite much activity in the Labour Party, assisted by some academics – no viable, robust and realistic alternative to CCT had been found. In addition, because the previous Conservative government had adopted a more consultative approach to the last phase of the extension to CCT, that for white-collar services, there was not felt to be the same urgency for repeal of the legislation.

The emergence of Best Value

Despite these problems, some three weeks after the election Hilary Armstrong, the Minister for Local Government, announced the first steps to replace CCT by stating the government's intention to place a duty on local authorities to secure 'Best Value', with changes to primary legislation being promised as soon as parliamentary time allowed. The government's initial steps were to introduce, for consultative purposes, 12 principles of Best Value, to establish the setting up of pilot projects, and to carry out a quick review of CCT to identify what short-term adjustments could be made which would not require primary legislation and would be consistent with the concept of Best Value principles.

THE 12 BEST VALUE PRINCIPLES

1. The duty of Best Value is one that local authorities will owe to local people, both as taxpayers and the customers of local authority services. Performance plans should support the process of local accountability to the electorate.
2. Achieving Best Value is not just about economy and efficiency, but also about effectiveness and the quality of local services – the setting of targets and performance against these should therefore underpin the new regime.
3. The duty should apply to a wider range of services than those now covered by CCT. Details will be worked up jointly with Departments, the Audit Commission and the LGA.
4. There is no presumption that services must be privatised, and once the regime is in place there will be no general requirements for councils to put their services out to tender, but there is no reason why services should be delivered directly if other more efficient means are available. What matters is what works.
5. Competition will continue to be an important management tool, a test of best value and an important feature in performance plans. But it will not be the only management tool and is not in itself enough to demonstrate that Best Value is being achieved.
6. Central government will continue to set the basic framework for service provision, which will in some areas as now include national standards.

7 Detailed local targets should have regard to any national targets, and to performance indicators and targets set by the Audit Commission in order to support comparative competition between authorities and groups of authorities.

8 Both national and local targets should be built on the performance information that is in any case needed by good managers.

9 Auditors should confirm the integrity and comparability of performance information.

10 Auditors will report publicly on whether Best Value has been achieved, and should contribute constructively to plans for remedial action. This will include agreeing measurable targets for improvement and reporting on progress against agreed plans.

11 There should be provision for intervention at the direction of the Secretary of State on the advice of the Audit Commission when an authority has failed to take agreed remedial action, or has failed to achieve realistic targets for improvement.

12 The form of intervention should be appropriate to the nature of failure. Where an authority has made limited use of competition, and as an exception to the usual rule, intervention may include a requirement that a service or services should be put to competition. Intervention might also take the form of a requirement that an authority should accept external management support, and may relate either to specific services, or to the core management of the council. (DETR, 1997)

The principles were accompanied by a provisional framework that councils were expected to develop in their pursuit of Best Value (see Figure 3.1). This framework, described as a 'performance management framework' in the later Green Paper (DETR, 1998a), consisted of a process or set of procedures that resulted from the 12 principles and the government's other statements on Best Value.

The principles were sufficiently broadly stated to suggest that the government's intention was to produce a regime that was less prescriptive and coercive than CCT but a succession of ministerial speeches demonstrated a pragmatic insistence that the regime must be successful – despite the fact that neither the principles, nor the subsequent Green Paper (DETR, 1998a) attempted to define Best Value in a substantive way. All government pronouncements related to the *process* by which it was to be achieved rather than to what it was. Despite the concept being something of a hollow one, a mint with the hole in the middle, government spokespersons left local

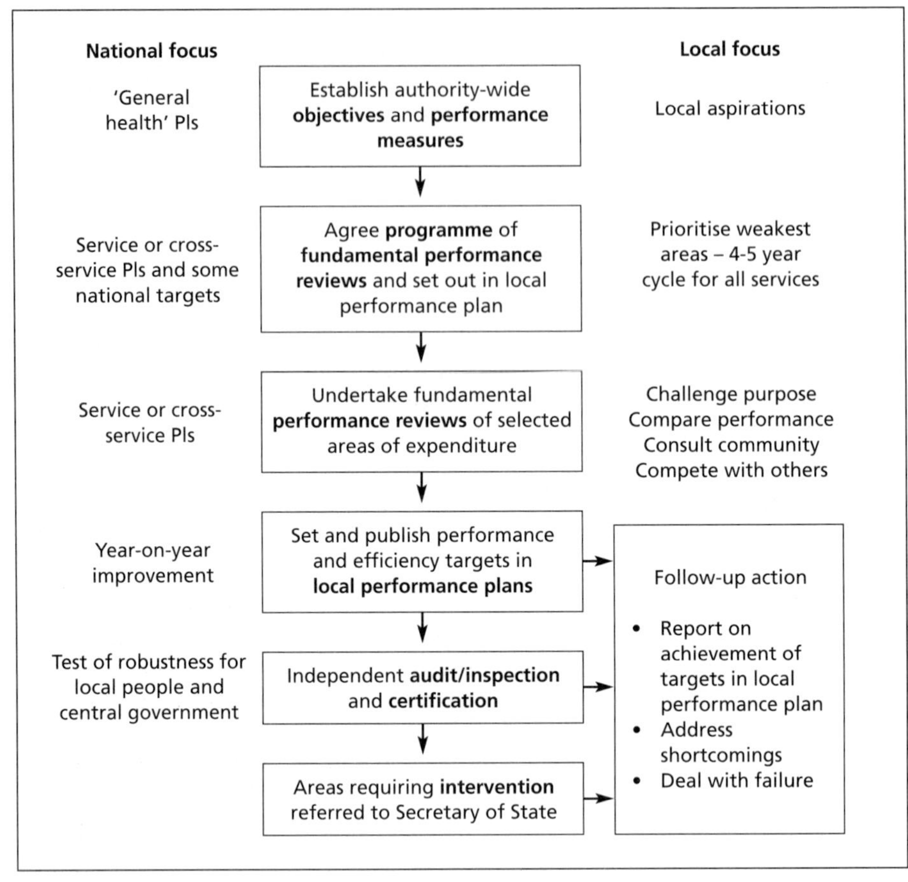

Figure 3.1 The Best Value performance management framework

Source: DETR – Modernising Local Government: Improving Local Services Through Best Value, 1998. Crown copyright is reproduced with the permission of the Controller of Her Majesty's Stationery Office.

authorities in no doubt that it had to be a success, threatening not simply the retention of CCT but a reduction in local democracy.

In February 1998 the Prime Minister's personal vision for local government directly addressed the issue of Best Value.

> *At the heart of the Best Value process will be four tools – the four Cs – which councils will use to make sure their services are of the highest quality:*
>
> - *challenging the underlying purpose, objectives, structures and costs of a service;*
> - *consulting with those who use services to make sure that they are responsive to their needs and concerns, and with those who provide them to tap their ideas for increasing the efficiency and quality of services;*
> - *comparing the performance of services with others, using performance indicators and benchmarking to see how improvements can be made; and*

- *competing with other providers to make sure that services are provided in the best way possible. (Blair, 1998)*

The Prime Minister also made clear that 'Best Value is not a short cut for getting out of CCT. Nor does it mean councils going soft on competition.' The government's Green Paper, published at around the same time, was equally clear that 'Competition will...continue to be an *essential* management tool for securing improvement' (DETR, 1998a, para 4.16). This is in contrast to its earlier statement of the 12 principles (see principle 5 above) in which it was described as an '*important* management tool'. The same paper went further down this path in stating that the government might consider issuing statutory guidance on good procurement or tendering practice and:

> *...could include a general presumption that services should be exposed periodically to competition except where authorities are able to argue convincingly why this is inappropriate. (DETR, 1998a, para 4.16)*

The Green Paper identified a number of new, proposed requirements to be placed on local authorities which closely followed the lines indicated in their 12 principles:

- *a duty on local authorities to obtain Best Value for the public;*
- *a provision to enable the appropriate Secretary of State to issue statutory guidance as to how authorities might comply with that duty;*
- *a requirement that authorities should carry out periodic reviews of their services in accordance with statutory guidance;*
- *a requirement that authorities should prepare and publish local performance plans, and powers to enable the Secretary of State to issue statutory guidance on the form, timing and content of such plans;*
- *a requirement that authorities should publish information on their performance against specific indicators laid down by the Secretary of State or the Audit Commission;*
- *a requirement that authorities should consult local taxpayers, the local business community and service users at key stages, particularly in setting targets to improve service performance, and to take account of any representations that they might receive in finalising their targets in their performance plans;*
- *a requirement that authorities should report back on their performance against targets;*
- *a requirement on external auditors to provide an opinion on (a) whether plans and attendant procedures are consistent with the provisions of the legislation and statutory guidance and regulations; and (b) whether local authority reports on performance against plans are accurate;*
- *a requirement that external auditors or inspectors should notify the appropriate Secretary of State where an authority has failed to meet its performance targets;*
- *a provision for the Secretary of State to take appropriate action in the case of persistent failure. (DETR, 1998a, para. 7.3)*

These requirements and the earlier 12 principles provided the basis on which the proposed Best Value pilot projects could proceed. Their evolution provides an interesting example of the way in which policy initiatives emerge and are subsequently developed in response to competing policy objectives. The greatest problem for local authorities in turning Best Value into a realistic tool for political and managerial decision making is its all-embracing nature. It requires local authorities to be far more analytically rigorous in reviewing their services within a more prescriptive regulatory regime.

The local government response

Local government, perhaps inspired by the anticipation of working with a non-Conservative government for the first time in 18 years, attracted by government statements of its intention to build a partnership with local government and exercised by simultaneous threats of the consequences of Best Value failing, responded very positively in attempting to unravel the Gordian knot that it presented. A joint statement from the Local Government Association (LGA), the Local Government Management Board (LGMB) and the main local government trade unions welcomed the proposals, emphasising the need for widespread consultation and for 'best employment practices' and noting the potential importance of the Single Status Agreement on employment. An LGMB/LGA Best Value partnership was created to co-ordinate their activities and the LGMB also produced its own publications to demonstrate what it could do to help local authorities (LGMB, 1997). The LGA later produced its own statement of six objectives for Best Value (LGA, 1998).

The pilot projects

The decision to set up pilot projects rather than to embark immediately on drafting new legislation has been a favoured approach of the new government in several areas of policy. The arrangements for establishing pilots differed in England, Scotland, Wales and Northern Ireland. In England, local authorities and police authorities were invited to submit bids to become pilot authorities. 152 submissions were made for pilot status and from these 35 local authority bids (some of which were joint and involved a total of 42 authorities) and two police authority bids were selected. The pilot projects were intended to commence by April 1998 and to run for a period of two to three years. The pilot authorities were offered exemption from the 1988 CCT legislation, but not from the original 1980 Act, and a further 16 authorities were encouraged to pursue their proposals outside of the formal pilot programme by being offered selective exemptions from CCT.

The pilot authorities did not form a representative sample in terms of type of authority, region or services included in the projects. Only about one quarter adopted a 'whole authority' approach with the remainder focusing only on selected services. Of more concern was the fact that only two intended to focus on regulatory services – the area which is likely to cause the greatest difficulty in applying Best Value concepts. Many pilots addressed traditional areas of service but others focused on particular client groups, on cross-cutting issues and on particular localities. (Martin, 1998)

The successful projects also appeared to vary in terms of the specificity of the processes they proposed to use. Several, such as Lewisham and Warwickshire, were based on existing frameworks such as the European Business Excellence Model (see Chapter 4 for further details). Others, such as Ipswich (see Figure 3.2) and Camden (see Figure 3.3) developed their own process frameworks.

What is Best Value?

At present, there is no clear definition of Best Value – nothing that goes beyond the concepts previously used to define 'performance' and 'value for money' (VFM).

The Labour Party's original proposals, published before the election, used five overlapping headings to describe Best Value.

- Fair employment – relating to the introduction of a minimum wage and the signing of the European Social Chapter.
- National and local standards – relating to a requirement to produce and adhere to local performance plans, the creation of a standards inspectorate, the need for monitoring and evaluation, and the requirement for external auditability.
- Promotion of active participation in service delivery.
- Openness, accountability and auditability – citizens juries etc.
- Fair trading – relating to cross-boundary trading and the production of trading accounts.

Several of these elements were apparently ignored after the election when statements by the DETR referred to the established performance concepts of economy, efficiency, effectiveness and quality. Filkin, in a document circulated to local authorities, used similar terminology:

> *Best value is the continuous search by a council to improve the quality, efficiency and effectiveness of all its activities for the public. (Filkin, 1997)*

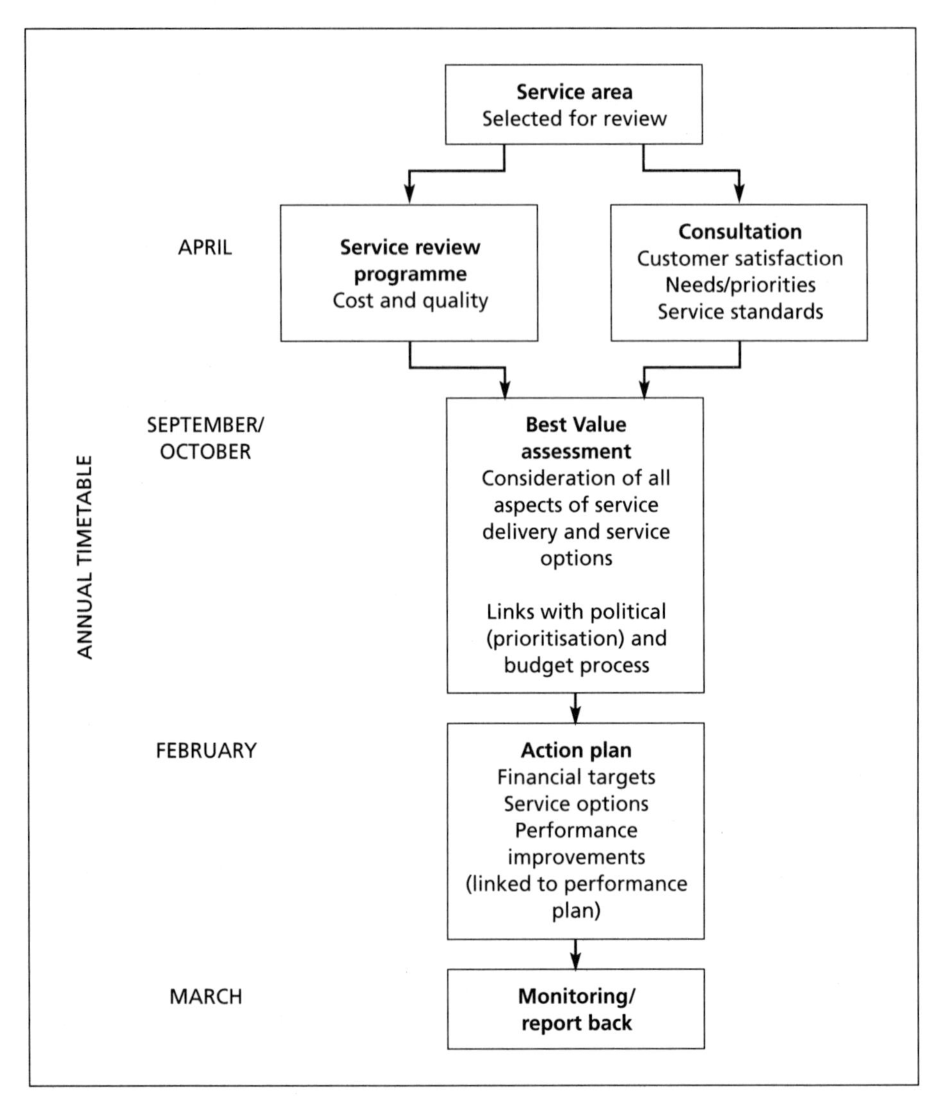

Figure 3.2 Best value process – Key elements

Source: Ipswich Borough Council – Best Value Pilot Bid, 1997

The reliance on old terminology suggests that Best Value could be no more than a continuation of the three 'E's approach pursued by the Audit Commission on behalf of Conservative governments, albeit dressed up with a new title to make it appear different. But a more detailed attempt to define Best Value was made by the Centre for Public Services. Concerned by the vague definition and the lack of references to equal opportunities and to social justice, the Centre proposed a seven part definition.

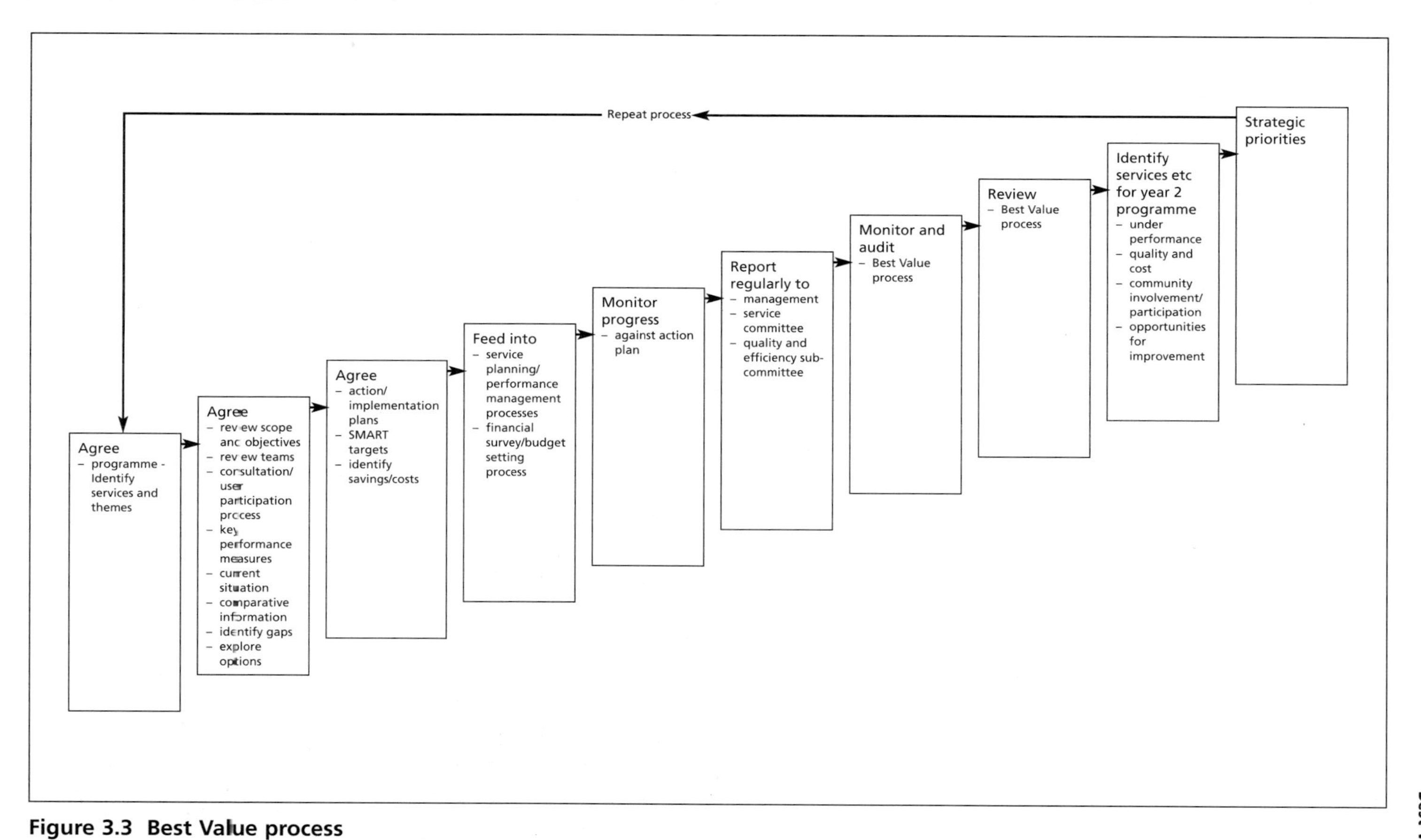

Figure 3.3 Best Value process

Source: London Borough of Camden – Best Value Pilot Bid, 1997

- **Quality of service** – this must be based on a comprehensive definition of quality which comprises eight elements covering the level and range of service, the service environment, the service relationship, quality of employment, accountability and democratic control of the service, management and organisation of the service, and monitoring and performance review... Each of these elements should have performance measures and targets based on national standards and priorities.
- **Achievement of sector/industry best practice** – the issue is not just the quality of service but whether the service incorporates best practice and innovation. ... Quality and best practice ... must be assessed together. One without the other is meaningless.
- **Quality of employment and training** – the quality of employment should cover maintaining national terms and conditions of service, implementation of the Single Status agreement, a national minimum wage, training and skill development, best practice equal opportunities policies, arrangements to secure health and safety for staff and users, and their inclusion in contract conditions for strategic sourcing of goods and services.
- **Implementation of corporate policies** – the implementation of corporate policies for equal opportunities, health and safety, environmental sustainability, community safety, public health, employment, anti-poverty strategies, regeneration of the local economy are a fundamental part of BV. This means setting annual performance measures and targets, and where quantification is difficult, detailed objectives.
- **Democratic accountability** – this should cover the democratic accountability of service provision to the authority and to users and that of the Best Value process itself.
- **Cost effectiveness** – this should be a balance between cost, quality, added value, the scope for continuous improvement in cost effectiveness and all the transaction costs of competition ... Cost effectiveness must also be examined in the context of service priorities.
- **Social and economic equity** – This should cover:
  - the extent to which the service meets social needs and the ability of the service to differentiate and target services to particular communities;
  - an assessment of the social value of improving the co-ordination and integration of particular service delivery systems;

- the contribution of the service to the local economy in terms of setting good employer and labour market standards;
- analysis of 'savings' from Best Value initiatives to identify corporate and public sector costs and benefits rather than simply focusing on the effect of service budgets. (Centre for Public Services, 1997)

It is also possible to express Best Value in terms of a policy and performance framework containing the following elements.

- A local authority's overall contribution to broad, national strategies such as (at the present time) social exclusion, lifelong learning and environmental sustainability.
- A local authority's democratic accountability in terms not just of the ballot box but the involvement and participation of service users, citizens, local communities, community based organisations and the business sector.
- A local authority's achievement of its own strategies, priorities and policies – which may in part reflect national strategies but may also include policies which are specifically shaped by local circumstances and politics. This may be termed *corporate policy effectiveness* and should include the effectiveness of those services purchased from outside organisations.
- The contribution of each individual local authority service to the achievement not only of its own strategies, aims and objectives, but also to corporate strategies and policies, and, where appropriate, to national strategies. This may be termed *service policy effectiveness and quality.*
- The *economy* with which services and goods are purchased from other organisations – including the full transaction costs involved in so doing.
- The *economy and efficiency* with which individual services are produced and delivered by the local authority.
- Finally, for any policies or services where it is agreed that it is not possible to directly assess issues of equity, economy, efficiency and effectiveness it may be necessary to provide a less quantitative form of analysis in the form of a commentary.

Best Value, contracting and competition

It has become clear that the government is not ideologically committed to in-house provision. Best Value places on councils the onus of demonstrating they can achieve the economic objectives of CCT without the compulsion to compete and that they can do so by using an approach which, by avoiding the transaction costs and other inefficiencies of CCT, could be a more efficient process while also allowing a greater focus on service quality and the needs and expectations of users and citizens.

In the private sector, the CCT approach to contracting – with potential contractors competing at arms length largely on price – has been rejected in favour of an approach which stresses the development of close relations between client and contractor and the creation of value in the supply chain by having an integrated system of clients, producers and end-users all working for their mutual advantage. With its emphasis on improving quality for all stakeholders, Best Value may be seen as an attempt to integrate the most useful elements of internally oriented quality management and performance management with new forms of externally oriented relational contracting. There is, however, a danger that the importance given to competition as a basic technique for achieving Best Value could be applied in a limiting way so as to prevent local authorities from adopting the best methods of service delivery.

The scope of Best Value

The government has made it clear that the duty to obtain Best Value will apply 'to all local authority services, including regulatory and enabling functions' (DETR, 1997). It will therefore apply to all services which were not included in the CCT legislation or were exempted for 'de minimis' reasons. It will cover all white-collar services, an area in which even the Conservative government had been proceeding with some caution, and will apply to services such as education and social services which have had little or no experience of CCT. More interestingly and problematically it will also apply to those enabling functions which involve local authorities working with other public, private and not-for-profit sector organisations. Examples include local housing companies, Private Finance Initiative projects and services externalised to Trusts such as residential homes. There is little reference to how Best Value will apply to these kinds of arrangements but the logic of the overall concept demands that they should not be exempted from the process.

The key stakeholders

As was the case with the notion of 'Value for Money', one of the key questions which will emerge when introducing the Best Value regime is not just **how** Best Value will be defined and evaluated but **who** will do so. Given that the notion of 'value' in relation to the processes of public policy making and service delivery is inevitably a complex one which will involve some degree of 'soft' subjective judgement as well as 'hard' quantitative evaluation, the real question will be: Whose value will count – and be counted – and in what context will it be regarded as 'best'? The respective power and roles of different stakeholders at each stage of the process will be critical in determining the outcome.

The provisional framework gives a clear indication of who the main stakeholders are intended to be.

- The government and its departments – in defining the legislative base, in setting national standards and targets, and in having the power to intervene where a council is deemed to have 'failed.'
- The Audit Commission, and the Accounts Commission in Scotland – who will have key roles in defining Best Value, in determining the process for achieving it and in defining some national or regional standards and targets on behalf of the government.
- The English, Scottish and Welsh local government associations – whom the Government has promised will play an active partnership role in the practical development of Best Value. Their precise roles are likely to differ however – as has already been illustrated by the different ways the pilot projects have been set up in the three regions.
- The District Auditor and auditing firms that audit local authorities – who will be responsible for validating the process and evaluating councils' performance. They are also likely to have some influence in prescribing the methods and approaches to be used in auditing Best Value.
- The researchers at Warwick and Cardiff Universities who have been engaged to monitor and evaluate the pilot projects in, respectively, England and Wales and whose evaluation frameworks, concepts and conclusions will help shape both the definition and the process.
- Local councillors who will, according to the provisional framework, have a duty placed on them to have an overview of the council's performance, to agree annual performance plans and to carry out fundamental reviews each year of the services specified in their plans.

- Local managers and professional and technical staff who will be required to support their councillors in carrying out their duties and responsibilities but will also, at a technical level, have an important role in innovating and developing methodologies for measuring, evaluating and reviewing policies and services.
- Users of services, who have been explicitly included in the preliminary framework, and who, as Filkin (1997) has indicated, can be included in every stage of the process.
- The business community and community organisations – who will be included in the consultation process.
- Employees and their trade unions. The role of trade unions is not made explicit in the preliminary framework although UNISON was involved in the selection of the pilot projects, and local authorities in making their bids were required to demonstrate that they had trade union support. The implementation of the concept of continuous improvement will be particularly dependent on employee and trade union support.

The growth of external auditing, inspecting and evaluation

Auditors were given a role in validating the bids for the pilot projects and it is clear that they will be given an enlarged and more powerful role in auditing and validating the Best Value process in each authority, including the validation of a local authority's use of individual evaluation and review techniques. The government has already indicated that new powers and resources may be needed for auditors. Depending on the extent of the additional powers given to the Audit Commission and to auditors, there are three issues of concern.

- If the notion of Best Value is to be developed in the holistic way suggested above then auditors will be required to make judgements about issues of policy effectiveness which may stretch them beyond the bounds of their professional training and competence.
- If, as the government has stated, Best Value is to include all local authority activities, then it must necessarily include those activities where local authorities are working in partnership with, or through contracts with, private sector organisations. It may therefore be necessary for the powers of the local authority's auditor to be extended to the investigation, evaluation and even auditing of the private sector organisation. Where the local authority and its private sector partner organisation are audited by

the same private sector auditing firm, conflicts of interest are likely to arise. The legislation on Best Value will need to make provision for dealing with such cases.

- As noted earlier, Best Value could be implemented in a manner which will accentuate the existing climate of external control and conformance – at the expense of local autonomy and ownership.

How can Best Value be made into a workable concept?

There are a number of issues which need to be addressed if Best Value is to become a workable process for both local and central government.

1 Overcoming the problems presented by the concepts of effectiveness and quality

Best Value has been described as involving effectiveness and quality as well as economy and efficiency. The analytical and information base for measuring and evaluating these dimensions of performance are variable but often underdeveloped. This is particularly true of effectiveness and quality although for basically different reasons. In the case of effectiveness, which is a concept which by definition must be based on the policy objectives of each local authority, there is a fundamental problem of constructing indicators which can be used on a comparative basis and, given that the theme of comparability has emerged strongly, this creates a problem. In the case of quality, the measurement problem is not so much one of comparability but of the multiple measures which are needed to address each dimension of the quality of each service. Forming judgements about quality will consequently involve making judgements against a range of quality criteria, some of which may be expressed as quantitative targets, others as quantitative standards and others as unquantified but qualitatively expressed criteria. Further research and technical experimentation is needed to develop more robust and reliable sets of effectiveness and quality measures.

2 Equity and equality

The application of the 3 'E's and quality to Best Value does not represent a significant step forward. They are the four main dimensions of performance which local and central government have been grappling with for many years. Depending on how they are defined, it may be argued that they omit other dimensions of performance of which the most important are equity and equality. As will be seen in Chapter 5, although it has been claimed that these dimensions cannot be measured, they can and are. If Best Value is to mean anything more than the existing term 'Value for Money', then equity and equality issues must occupy a central position in the definition of 'Value.'

3 Outcomes and processes

There is a strong theme running through Best Value pointing to the importance of focusing on outputs and outcomes and away from inputs and process. This theme is an important one but can sometimes obscure the fact that process and outcome can be inextricably linked. This becomes clear when the concept of equity is explored. One definition of equity relates to the equity with which people in similar situations are treated and the treatment of individuals is a constituent part of the process of providing the service. This gives rise to the concept of 'due process' and it is this aspect of performance which is most frequently the subject of investigations by the Local Government Ombudsman. 'Due process' is fundamental to equity and therefore to Best Value but it cannot be measured by focusing exclusively on the outcome of service delivery.

4 Alternative methods of service delivery

The increased importance attached to competition and market testing presents two problems. The first is that there are some local authority services for which no real market place exists – thereby making it difficult or impossible to use this approach as part of the review process. The second problem is that competition in the form of CCT has taken away from local government the critical strategic decision of which method of service delivery is most appropriate for each service. The decision has, in effect, been made for them by the legislation by limiting the choice to in-house delivery or to an external contract obtained by using a formal competitive process. The only strategic choice for the local authority was how strongly it wished to compete to retain the in-house delivery mode.

However, there are many alternative methods of service delivery. The Plunkett Foundation (1993), for example, identified 19 options under 7 headings: local authority led, investor led, employee led, customer led, management led, community benefit organisations and 'hybrid' models. The achievement of Best Value may largely be determined by the ability to select the 'best' option for service delivery and what is best will vary for each service and each locality. There needs to be built into the Best Value framework an explicit process of **options appraisal** in which local authorities consider and make the strategic choice about which options are available and appropriate. This process will require the development of an appraisal framework which identifies the key factors that need to be considered.

Such a framework can be developed from existing frameworks such as that developed by the Plunkett Foundation (1993) which includes decision criteria relating to: the characteristics of the service; business performance; the resources involved; the interests of stakeholders; financial constraints; and corporate strategy. Thomas and Puffitt (1997) have also produced a framework of contingency factors that include: the regulations which apply to the service; the characteristics of the service; the interests and circumstances of users; the restraints and opportunities for partnership working; the characteristics of potential providers; and the market conditions. Concepts drawn from business investment analysis techniques might also contribute to such a framework.

5 *A stakeholder approach to Best Value*

References to 'stakeholding' were an important element of the rhetoric of the Labour Party prior to the election but have since become less pronounced. Nonetheless an examination of the Best Value framework (Figure 3.1) reveals that, as has already been noted, there has been a real attempt to build in the views of a variety of stakeholding groups. There is a danger however that the framework will be implemented in a way which increases rather than decreases the relative power of different groups. The good intentions with respect to the involvement of service users and the community may count for little unless the criteria they use in making judgements about services are made explicit and given an appropriate weighting in relation to the predominantly financial and economic criteria used by the Audit Commission and auditors.

6 *A market test and a community test*

If Best Value is viewed primarily as a replacement for CCT then it is likely to be achieved primarily through mechanisms which seek to compare a local authority's performance with that which has been or can be achieved elsewhere in the market. That, almost inevitably, will lead to a continuing focus on costs, economy and productivity. However, as the framework attempts to demonstrate, the need for input from service users and the wider community should create a 'community test' of local authority performance as well as a 'market test.' The main difficulty in achieving this will be in devising methodologies and evaluative criteria which result in appropriate, and perhaps equal, weight being given to the two tests, particularly as one will produce more quantitative 'hard' data and the other 'softer', qualitative data.

7 A centralising or a decentralising process?

In Chapter 2 attention was drawn to the centralising tendencies of successive Conservative governments in the 1980s and 1990s. While it is too early to make any absolute judgements of the Labour government in this respect, it is necessary to be clear whether the intention or the effect of the Best Value process will be to centralise power in central government and its agencies or to decentralise decision-making power to local authorities.

8 An analytical focus on services or on policies

The language of the Best Value framework is expressed in terms of services but an alternative focus of attention would be to make policies the building bricks of the analytical review process. A focus on services is more likely to lead to a focus on economy and efficiency, processes and inputs – particularly where services remain delivered in-house.

9 Differentiating services.

Given that the Best Value process is to be applied to all services, the question arises of whether all services can use the same analytical and review processes or whether they need to be differentiated into categories each of which uses a different process. Services can be differentiated along several dimensions – resourcing, relationship with client, public or private benefit, etc. – and by whether they exist within full market, quasi-market or non-market conditions. Some of these dimensions are likely to have an impact on the approach needed to carry out fundamental reviews.

Conclusion

Best Value represents, for all its current uncertainties, the most holistic framework yet developed within which local authorities can continue to develop their approaches to performance and quality management in a way which may involve creating a more participative form of local democracy. However, because the government's framework has a combination of permissive, prescriptive and regulatory elements built into it, its real value will be dependent on the way in which these elements are balanced against each other in practice.

4

Concepts, pictures and stories of performance

Introduction

The purpose of this chapter is to provide a pause before proceeding to the chapters that examine the detail of performance management. It does so by briefly outlining the three most basic concepts associated with performance management – models of rational, systems decision making; motivation theory; and quality management concepts – and by considering some broader issues concerning the reporting of performance.

The rational, systems model of decision making

Performance management is founded on a 'rational' model which views organisational decision making as a single, closed loop. The model has been formulated with numerous variations and degrees of sophistication but for a local authority can be expressed as follows.

- **Step 1 Analysis of environmental and community needs** – the starting point for decision making is to undertake a full analysis of local needs.
- **Step 2 Resource analysis** – the available and potentially available resources need to be identified.
- **Step 3 Strategies** – the authority next can determine its objectives and strategies in the light of the needs, resources and its political aims.
- **Step 4 Planning** – strategies are then turned into action plans and development plans for services and for all types of resource utilisation.
- **Step 5 Targets and standards** – plans need to be expressed in terms of precise targets, standards and indicators which can be used for monitoring performance.

- **Step 6 Action** – the organisation can now proceed with providing services.
- **Step 7 Monitoring** – actual performance against plan and the validity of the plan are continuously monitored using the specified targets, standards and indicators.
- **Step 8 Review and evaluation** – the results of monitoring are used to periodically review both performance and plans and the results fed back into the next round of decision making, thereby closing the loop.

It will be readily apparent that this is an extremely oversimplified model of reality which ignores as much as it expresses. It has been criticised on many grounds, the most important of which are that:

- it does not sufficiently recognise the political and power dimensions of decision making;
- it assumes that organisations and individuals act in an accordance with its own view of 'rationality';
- it fails to recognise that in most circumstances information is partial rather than complete and that reviews and evaluations will also therefore be incomplete;
- it assumes the existence of a degree of certainty and stability which rarely exists.

However, it is the model on which not just performance management but also business planning and strategic management frameworks are based. Many of the changes and developments in local authority decision making can be regarded as an attempt to implement at least an approximation of the model.

Theories of motivation

It does not require a great theorist to recognise that people are motivated by different circumstances. Most casual observers of the human condition can also perceive that motivations can change during a person's life. They will also recognise that human motivation is fundamental to individual and organisational success. But knowing exactly how individuals are, or are not, motivated is much more complex and is not necessarily made easier by the existence of an ever increasing number of theories. What conclusions and practical advice can be drawn from them?

The first general lesson is that many of the so-called 'theories' lack sufficient supporting empirical evidence. Many managers, as part of their initial management training, will have learned about Maslow's Hierarchy of Needs or Hertzberg's Two Factor theory, and some will have had these theories presented to them as absolute 'truths'. But when researchers have attempted to produce empirical evidence the results have been very mixed. There are as many research studies which disprove or fail to support Hertzberg's theory as there are ones supporting it.

The second thing to learn is that psychological (and perhaps other) theories do not have to be empirically proven for them to be enormously influential in the workplace. Despite the lack of clear empirical evidence supporting Hertzberg's Two Factor theory, it nonetheless became one of the most influential theories of the 1960s and, directly and indirectly, gave rise to an industry of job improvement and job enlargement schemes which did result in many practical benefits for both employees and employers.

The third learning point is that everybody is a 'theorist' in the sense that they conduct their relationships with other people on the basis of a set of assumptions which may amount to an implicit theory. Organisations also have theories, or at least sets of assumptions, about human motivation which are used as the basis for designing procedures for managing staff, and these theories may be explicit or implicit. A great deal of management practice is focused on the eternal problem of how to produce the circumstances which ensure that people work together in pursuit of goals which are important to each person as well as the organisation. Management therefore involves trying to understand why people behave in the way they do, how they can be influenced to behave in different ways, and how their behaviour can be predicted in the future.

Performance management, in its practical application, may not appear to be based on any explicit motivation theories – but it is. Three theories have been dominant in shaping and developing performance management: Expectancy theory, Goal-setting theory and Reinforcement theory and these are presented and discussed in Chapter 6 in relation to the management of the performance of individuals.

Quality Management

Approaches to the management of quality have developed in a number of ways but owe much of their initial success to early writers such as Deming and Juran. Based originally on experience in Japan when that country was regarded as the dominant force in manufacturing, many of the techniques developed, such as 'Just-in-Time' and Total Quality Management (TQM), were based on two complementary approaches – one being an analytical, measurement-driven approach to defining and producing quality at a given cost, the other being the development of a culture which encouraged and enabled all employees to contribute to both quality and efficiency. Despite the difficulty in maintaining an appropriate balance between these two approaches, Quality Management has become a dominant approach in both the private and public sectors. In local government it has been the source of numerous changes to the way in which employees are managed and services designed and delivered. Quality assurance and control, quality circles, benchmarking, charters and standards, continuous improvement programmes and process mapping have all emerged from the 'quality movement'.

The Business Excellence model developed by the European Foundation for Quality Management (EFQM) is closely linked to TQM and has been introduced into several local authorities such as Cheshire and Southwark – with beneficial results. Several of the submissions for Best Value pilot project status proposed to use the model as a fundamental part of their approach. The model (illustrated in Figure 4.1) can be used as a self-evaluation tool and sets the criteria for the UK Quality Award. It offers a comprehensive and coherent way of showing the principal factors that are claimed to contribute to organisational success and has been adapted for use in local government. It is likely that its use will become more widespread and will, as a result, provide a basis for local authorities to benchmark themselves in relation to the specified criteria.

In many respects 'quality' and 'performance' have become two of the most frequently used words in the vocabulary of public service management and there is a close but sometimes uneasy and unclear relationship between the two. Some local authorities, in describing their management systems have preferred to use the term 'quality', which they see as having more positive connotations than 'performance', although in practice what they do under the banner of quality may be little different to what other authorities refer to as performance. Other authorities, having had less than encouraging results from applying the simple and sometimes crude approaches to performance management that were used in the 1980s, made a very determined attempt to apply different styles drawn from the quality movement.

The result is that it is now difficult to distinguish some quality led systems from those that are performance led. There has been a fusing of the two approaches with performance management borrowing a great deal from quality management. There is little doubt, however, that there has been more creativity in the name of quality than in that of performance.

Quality has an engaging characteristic which has been successfully used, knowingly or intuitively, to persuade both public and private sector

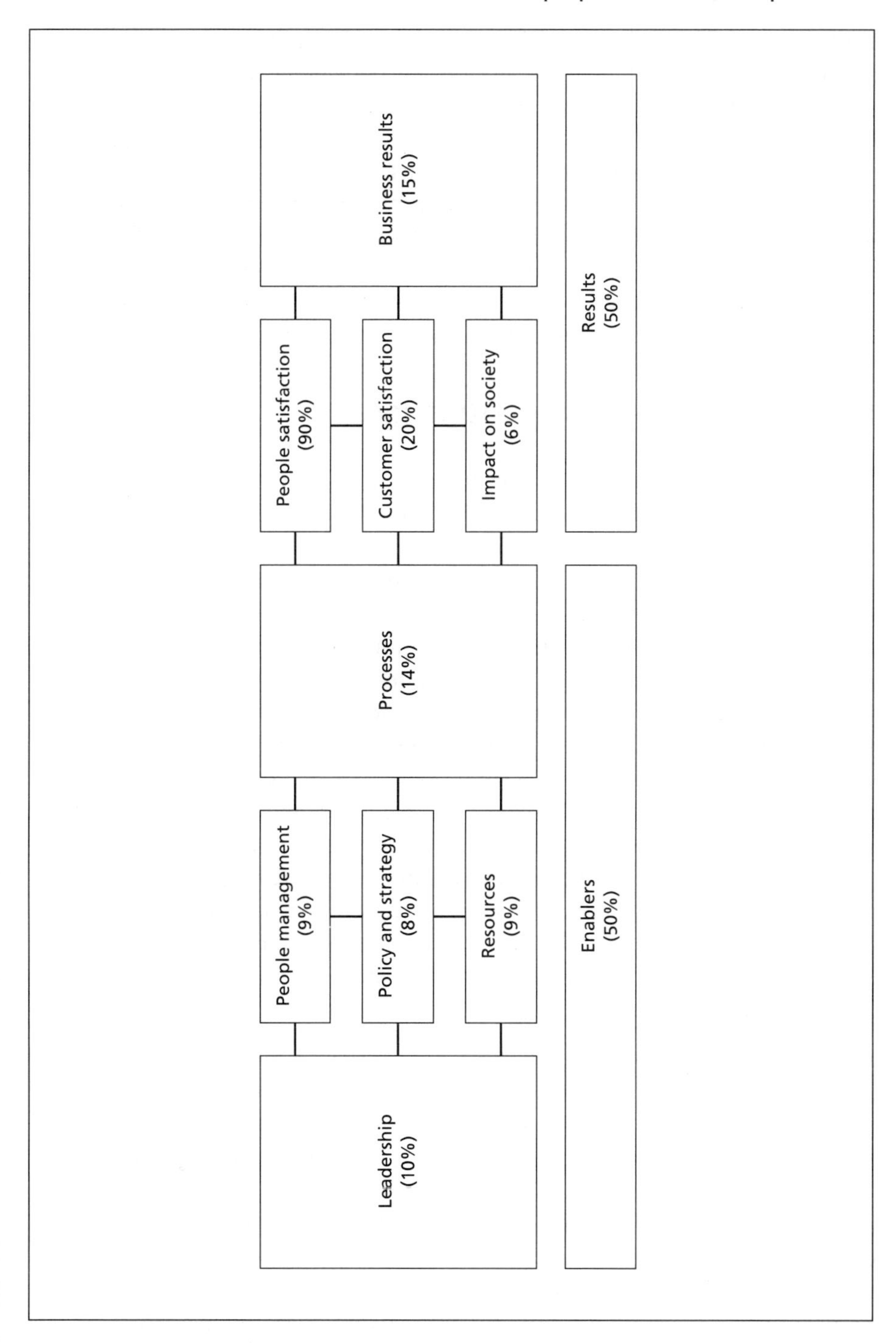

Figure 4.1 The Business Excellence model

Source: British Quality Foundation (copyright)

employees to change their working methods and conditions. For public sector employees, the prevailing 'performance' message in the 1980s of greater economy and efficiency was something that was difficult to fully engage with. Most people do not hold economy or efficiency as primary personal goals – although they may recognise that they are a necessary part of organisational life. They do not go home at the end of a good day's work and say to their friends or family – 'I had a great day today – I was really economic.' When they do experience satisfaction from their work it is far more likely to be associated with quality. Few people argue with the need for 'quality' but some may be less certain about 'performance'.

Pictures and stories of performance

It is also worth pausing to consider the type and nature of the pictures that are painted and the stories that are told about the performance of a local authority. In the same way as pictures come in different styles – impressionist, romantic-nationalist, surrealistic – and stories come in different forms – biography, novel, history – so the performance reports of a local authority come in different styles and formats. And as with pictures and stories, different styles and formats appeal to different people. In art and literature the fact that we have different forms and styles is generally valued as enriching our culture. There is generally no attempt, except in certain dictatorships, to impose a single story or a single style of picture. But is there a danger that in local government we are moving to a situation where only one form of story is valued and permitted? Performance management, coupled with central government's desire to retain tight control of local government, can lead to a situation where only one form of account is deemed to be legitimate – the account which is expressed statistically in the shape of a predetermined and externally prescribed set of performance indicators.

Pictures, stories and accounts of a local authority's performance are not just recorded in performance indicators – they are told in Annual Reports which vary significantly in their content and style , in committee reports, and in the way the authority communicates with users, citizens and council tax payers. There are also the stories which are told in the local pub, in the party political meeting, in the community action group meeting and at the professional conference. These stories often rely more on the qualitative experiences of the storyteller than they do on any 'official' account. The stories vary not just in terms of their style and form but also in the values, perceptions and explanations of the storyteller. A local authority, if it is to improve its performance, has to take account of all of these different stories and pictures – and therein lies an enormous problem It requires the production of pictures and stories of performance for different audiences and different purposes and which satisfy different tastes and needs.

Consider a story of performance in another arena. Theatre critics provide us with performance reports. In part they may be written for the performers themselves as a form of feedback but their more ostensible purpose is to provide potential customers with evaluative information to use in deciding whether to attend the performance. Consider the following account written in the statistical, formal, objective style typical of so many local authority performance reports. Would it help you decide whether you should become a customer or not?

> *Play 'x' was performed by 'y' theatre company at 'z' theatre last night. 12 actors were employed to play 19 roles (representing an efficient use of thespian resources) on a stage measuring 'b' metres. It was performed in front of 'c' customers (64% capacity utilisation) with production costs of £d and box office income of £e. The play was performed as fully specified in the programme with the exception of its overrunning by three minutes and 25 seconds (a 2% overrun on stated completion target). The performance was followed by 2.47 minutes of applause.*
>
> *P.S. The theatre company has stated that the adverse weather last night was the primary reason for the company's failure to meet its capacity utilisation target of 80%. However because the existence of the wrong sort of weather is not a controllable factor, the company does not consider itself accountable for its failure.*

All pictures, stories and reports of performance are by nature selective. To provide a 'full' description of every facet of a play would entail the use of extensive narrative and statistical information. To fully describe and analyse the performance of even simple performances, such as the laying of a length of kerbstone, requires different perspectives on the story. To record the performance of social workers in terms of their perseverance, ingenuity, influence and persuasion, and their skilful acquisition and packaging of limited resources – in order to satisfy the quality of life needs of physically handicapped, isolated elderly people – would require a much fuller and more rounded story.

Because most stories are necessarily selective, they frequently tell us as much about the interests and objectives of the person who did the selection as they do about the nature of the performance itself. Central government and its agencies select the performance stories they want told about local government. Councillors select the performance stories to be told about their chief officers who in turn are instrumental in selecting the accounts which are told about their staff. At every stage of performance there is a process of selection, each selector using different criteria. There is little wonder that both front-line staff and customers and citizens sometimes stare in disbelief at the stories they read and the pictures they see painted – 'I just don't believe it!'

All those who have the power to select the stories, pictures and accounts of performance that are produced also have a responsibility for ensuring that those accounts are fit-for-purpose.

5

Managing by numbers

Introduction

The purpose of this chapter is to explore the principles and concepts which have informed the development and use of performance measurement in local government in recent years, with particular reference to the introduction and use of the Citizens Charter Performance Indicators and the future development of Best Value.

Management by number has become an increasingly attractive proposition for politicians and managers struggling to make sense of the complex, fast-changing world of public policy, as well as a tool for auditing and inspection agencies. In addition, successive governments are using selected performance targets as a way of stimulating and controlling local authorities. Management and government by number have so infused the thinking and practices of both central and local government that they represent a major shift in approach to public services. To some extent the same transformation has taken place in the private sector and it is interesting to note that many of the same issues and problems arise in both sectors. There can now be very few employees in the public sector whose work is not measured by the use of performance indicators which are either internally specified or are part of a nationally determined set of indicators. It was not always thus. Until recently, many councillors, managers and their staff appeared to be fundamentally opposed to any form of measurement – and particularly to the comparative use of performance indicators. The argument often went as follows: 'We can see that it is possible to measure other people's or organisations' work but *our* work just cannot be reduced to simple numbers – its far too complex, subtle and individualised.'

That kind of argument is now heard less frequently. Some people may still believe it but they have learned that there is little point in expressing it. The debate about performance measurement has moved on. The question is no longer *whether* performance should be measured but rather:

- *What* aspects of performance should be measured?
- *Who* should decide and use the measures?
- *How*, and by whom, should they be used?

A measurement revolution?

In 1991, Robert Eccles maintained that there had been a 'measurement revolution' in America. His 'performance measurement manifesto' begins:

> *Revolutions begin long before they are officially declared. For several years senior executives in a broad range of industries have been rethinking how to measure the performance of their businesses. They have recognised that new strategies and competitive realities demand new measurement systems. Now they are deeply engaged in defining and developing those systems for their companies.* (Eccles, 1991)

The article ends:

> *Finally, recognise that once begun, this is a revolution that never ends. We are not simply talking about changing the basis of performance measurement from financial statistics to something else. We are talking about a new philosophy of performance measurement that regards it as an ongoing, evolving process. And just as igniting the revolution will take special effort, so will maintaining its momentum and reaping the rewards in the years ahead.* (Eccles, 1991)

Despite the somewhat hyperbolic language it could as easily have been written about local government in the 1980s and 1990s. Even models of British reserve such as Peter Jackson have acknowledged that performance measurement is at the crossroads of becoming one of the 'big issues' (Jackson, 1995). There has been a revolution: spearheaded by legislation, supported by the Audit Commission and the inspection agencies and used by a new breed of national and local politicians, who considered that performance indicators (and particularly their expression in the form of **targets**) were effective tools for making the institutions of national and central government respond to their political objectives in a way they had failed to do in the past. Some managers, faced with this new style of political management, and also faced with increased public expectations at a time of resource constraint, also began to regard performance measures and targets as an effective instrument of 'hands-off' managerial and political control

The local government response

It is apparent that some authorities, independently of the governmental pressures, have for a number of years used a highly quantitative approach based on the specification and use of their own sets of performance indicators. The London Borough of Bexley – one of the first authorities to implement performance management systems in the early 1980s – included as a central part of its approach a set of performance indicators for every service. Other authorities such as Redditch District Council and the Royal Borough of Windsor and Maidenhead also developed a style of management in which performance indicators played a major role. The London Borough of Brent has also extensively developed the use of indicators as part of its performance review process. Many other authorities which had not traditionally developed such an approach were encouraged to do so, as the pressures of statutory requirements to publish performance indicators, continuing resource constraint and the rising demand for services became more acutely felt. Struggling to make more reasoned and justified decisions as to where spending cuts should fall and small amounts of growth applied, committee reports contained more and more statements of the following kind.

In future, if growth bids are to succeed, we will have to demonstrate that previous allocations have been wisely spent and that new demands have a proven need. Also, we will have to provide evidence of the measures that we will use to monitor the operation of any new scheme. (Report by a senior social services manager to his staff)

The broader issues

Despite the extent to which performance indicators and targets are used there remain a number of broad issues requiring consideration (which are discussed in more detail below):

- the performance measurement battleground
- performance measurement and power
- the comprehensiveness versus selectivity paradox
- targets versus indicators
- from assertion to demonstration
- criteria first – measurement second
- desperately seeking solutions
- don't reduce me to an indicator.

The performance measurement battleground

Too often discussions about performance measurement slip into two equally extreme and ultimately indefensible camps. On the one hand there are the proponents of measurement who not only see it as the main political and managerial tool for directing and controlling the performance of public policy but are largely blind to its limitations and inconsistencies. For them, the process of measurement is a logical and objective route to better government and management. They will tend to note with uncritical approval that 'what gets measured gets done' and that 'what is counted is what counts'.

On the other hand are the opponents who can see nothing but the dangers and imperfections of any attempt to measure the performance of public services. Because, they will argue, all measurement is imperfect and incomplete, lacking sufficient reliability, validity and robustness, measures should either not be used at all or with the utmost caution. If you cannot measure everything which is relevant in a reliable, valid and consistent way then you should measure nothing for fear of distorting the 'picture of performance' in an unacceptable and dangerous way.

These opponents base their arguments on three grounds. First there are technical arguments about the inevitable flaws, inconsistencies and incompleteness of all sets of performance indicators; then there are arguments relating to the improper or injudicious use of performance indicators; and finally there are concerns which are rarely explicitly voiced but which essentially relate to the shift in power between different stakeholder groups which can be achieved by measuring performance and by placing the results in the public arena.

There is also an even more fundamental challenge to performance measurement from writers such as Walsh (1992).

> *It is not axiomatic that we should measure the performance of public service agencies at all. It may be impossible to do so, or the cost may not be worth the outcome. It makes perfect sense to say that it is worth providing a particular service in a particular way because it may have a beneficial effect, even though it may not be possible, either before or after the event to determine whether or not it actually worked. (Walsh, 1992)*

In the middle ground there are a large number of commentators who recognise that performance measurement is a necessary but imperfect tool of management – a tool which creates particular problems when applied to the public sector. Performance has been described as a 'slippery' (Jackson, 1995) and 'elusive' concept (Stewart and Walsh, 1995). It is also regarded as multi-functional and complex. If the concept of performance has such characteristics then inevitably attempts to measure it will be imperfect.

Performance measurement and power

Using measurement to shift the balance of power between public sector managers and professionals, between front-line-staff and management, between councillors and officers, between local and central politicians, between local authorities and government departments and – perhaps most crucially – between the institutions of government and public service providers on the one hand and citizens and communities on the other, has been a fundamental objective of past and current reforms. It underpins so many legislative and regulatory changes that it is now central to the way in which we conduct the affairs of the British State, nationally, regionally and locally.

This use of performance measurement is not just expressed through the more obvious developments, such as the Citizens Charter indicators, but also in the contracts for the newly created government agencies, through the quantitative specifications of performance in the increasing number of internal and external contracts which have proliferated in the public sector, in the use of specific performance indicators and objectives used for specific funding programmes such as SRB (Single Regeneration Budget) and in the increasing tendency for ministers to announce specific quantitative targets for their new policy initiatives. But any attempt to alter the balance of power will not go unchallenged. Public sector managers still retain considerable power in determining how the performance of their services is measured and this has led one commentator to suggest that it is necessary to move 'beyond the managerial model of performance measurement' (Pollitt, 1986).

The comprehensiveness versus selectivity paradox

If the main purpose of measuring performance is to highlight those aspects of performance that are of particular relevance and importance to managers, politicians or the public, then a very limited number of performance indicators is needed in order to ensure that each one is suitably prominent and provides a focus for attention. However, if it is accepted that local authority performance is a complex, multi-dimensional concept, then it is apparent that very large numbers of indicators are needed to obtain a complete picture of performance. This results in a genuine paradox – the greater the selectivity the greater the focus but, at the same time, the less likely it will be that the performance indicators reflect all the important dimensions of performance – and vice versa.

One possible solution to this paradox is to use a limited number of performance measures as performance *targets* in those areas where it is considered that performance needs to be improved, supported by a larger number of performance *standards* for other significant dimensions of performance. In adopting such an approach, the main issues for debate will centre on the extent to which particular targets and/or standards should be set locally or nationally but there is plenty of evidence that in recent years successive governments have increased the number of both. The present government has already indicated its intention to extend the role of the Audit Commission to include the setting of national standards.

Targets versus indicators

The most dramatic shift has been in the use of individual measures of performance as *targets* to be achieved rather than as *indicators* which are used for evaluative purposes. This has been a trend not only in central government but also amongst local authorities. The potential power of targets is considerable in that they constitute public political and managerial promises of what will be achieved in the future. The evaluative use of indicators, although theoretically important, tends to have less impact in practice either because evaluation is not undertaken or because such indicators, even when available, are often not brought to bear on the evaluation process. They rarely therefore have the same impact as targets.

The increased use of quantitative targets is of profound importance for public policy and management for three principal reasons. First, as was noted above, it is an attempt to change the balance of power between different stakeholder groups. Targets can be used as control mechanisms and are made even more powerful when they form part of reward and punishment systems, as in the case of performance related pay, or when they are related to the future funding of the organisation as a whole. The second reason is that they are the dominant symbol of a more business oriented style of public policy making in which 'results' have become more important than 'process'. In contrast to the Bananarama hit-song 'It's not what you do it's the way that you do it' the reality of public life is increasingly that 'it's what you do that counts.' The third reason is the most worrying. If it is accepted that the performance of public policies and public services can be measured in many different ways then the selection of just one or two measures as targets can result in extreme distortions in what is achieved. Where performance measures are used as targets they must reflect, in a balanced way, the most important outcomes and effects of a policy.

Targets are powerful instruments of *focus* – that is their fundamental purpose – they focus organisational and individual thinking, effort and energy on their achievement. By so doing they distract thinking, effort and energy from those things which are not expressed as targets. Within this dilemma lies both the power and the damage that can result from their use. Too few targets is likely to cause policy and service distortions while too many targets causes confusion, overload and lack of clear focus and direction.

From assertion to demonstration

Local authority managers have often, in the past, made assertions to their elected members that the services they manage are economic, efficient and effective but without providing evidence with which councillors can test out the assertion. Without evidence, councillors are in a position where they can either accept the assertion, challenge it but without substantive evidence to support their challenge, or, most commonly, challenge it with anecdotal information they have acquired themselves – evidence which itself can be challenged because it is merely anecdotal and incidental and does not therefore represent the full 'picture'. Supporting assertion with quantified performance information begins to shift the balance of power between manager and councillor. But not by a great deal if it is the manager who is deciding what performance information is to be presented – for in so doing the manager is determining the criteria by which the performance can be judged. Only when the councillor specifies the performance data does the balance of power really begin to shift.

Criteria first – measurement second

There have been many attempts to develop indicators but these have generally proceeded in an upside-down manner. Taking an understandably pragmatic approach, organisations look at what data they currently possess, and perhaps at what data they could easily produce in the future, to see what performance indicators can be constructed. This invariably produces an incomplete and confusing set of indicators. The alternative way to proceed is to first identify the criteria that should be used to judge a policy or a service. Performance measures, indicators or targets are simply quantified expressions of the *criteria* of performance that we wish to use. Some criteria will be more easily measured than others. Some ways of measuring certain criteria will be more expensive than others. And some criteria may have no obvious way of being measured.

The 'model' rational process is therefore as follows.

- Establish the criteria of performance to be used.
- Identify different ways of measuring each criteria.
- Where more than one measure has been identified for each criteria, select the most important.
- Where a large number of measures have been identified for a policy or a service, select a limited number which are deemed to be the most significant and important, ensuring that every criteria still has one measure related to it.

- Examine your existing data systems to find out whether they contain the data needed to construct the measures you have selected.
- If it is not possible to produce the measures you need with your existing data systems, improve, redesign or replace them with systems which will.

This purist approach may sound like a counsel of perfection but it is in fact the process which many new DSOs have been through in order to create the kind of performance information they need to survive.

Desperately seeking solutions

The prevailing culture of measurement has led some managers into a desperate search for performance indicators – a search which is characterised as much by its randomness as its orderliness. The quest has been supported by the tendency of some commentators to produce extensive lists of indicators, an example of which is 'Municipal benchmarks' (Ammons, 1996). A thick, weighty tome it contains just 22 pages of analysis of the concept of performance measurement followed by 266 pages of list after list of the performance measures used by individual municipalities in America – interspersed with only the briefest of commentary. The purpose of the lists is not clear but it must be assumed that it is to enable municipal managers to randomly select measures for their own use.

The same approach appears to have been used in some local authorities, with managers and councillors basing their choice of performance indicators largely on what they currently have available or what has been imposed on them by external bodies, without any clear overview of what the resulting set of indicators adds up to.

Don't reduce me to an indicator

The final issue relates to those employees who perceived that the early and crude attempts to develop performance indicators had the effect of reducing the totality of their expertise, skill, dedication, experience, energy, ingenuity and application (in other words, all those attributes by which they define the value of their work both to themselves and to their organisation) to a single number. It may be countered that organisations have other mechanisms for valuing and rewarding their staff but the experience of many staff was that 'what counts is what is counted'. If the performance indicator was an efficiency indicator, or a volume indicator, or a speed of response indicator, then in reality that was *the* criteria by which they were judged. Given that many of the early sets of indicators were drawn up primarily on the basis of what data happened to be available, many staff found that the value of their work was being judged by criteria of doubtful validity.

The criteria to be used in measuring performance – concepts and frameworks

The basic model of performance criteria which has been consistently applied to local government since the early 1980s has been the Audit Commission's specification of the 3 'E's – economy, efficiency and effectiveness.

The three concepts are based on a simple *input* (resources) *output* (volume of service produced) *impact/outcome* (the results or consequences) model of the process of producing public services, with economy relating to the procurement of inputs, or resources, efficiency being a ratio of the inputs to outputs and effectiveness being the relationship between service outputs and their impact or outcome. The three concepts were defined more precisely as follows.

Economy	Ensuring that assets and services are procured and maintained at the lowest possible cost consistent with a specified quality and quantity.
Efficiency	Providing a specified volume and quality of service with the lowest level of resources capable of meeting that specification.
Effectiveness	Providing the right services to enable a local authority to implement its policies and objectives.

These terms have been in regular use since the early 1980s but they remain poorly understood and are often given varying interpretations. The problems of understanding and interpretation stem from four causes. First, there are differences between the way in which some of the terms are technically defined and how they are used in common parlance. For example, when the term 'economic' is used to describe a local authority or a service it tends to mean cheap or low cost – neither of which correspond to the 'technical' definition above. Being 'economical with the truth' raises even further doubts about usage.

Second, there is the problem that at least one of the concepts has many different technical definitions. A rapid trawl of the performance measurement literature reveals at least nine types of efficiency: input-mix efficiency, productive efficiency, technical efficiency, output-mix efficiency, X-efficiency, allocative efficiency, horizontal target efficiency, vertical target efficiency and Pareto-efficiency. Some of these definitions are similar or even identical to each other but others represent quite different notions of the general concept. It is, as a consequence, not surprising that some people, including those who are using the terminology of the 3 'E's, become confused regarding the meaning they attach to the word. It may, however, be argued that fundamentally there are just two notions of efficiency: productive efficiency, which corresponds to the Audit Commission's definition, and allocative efficiency, which economists use to express the relationship between the costs and benefits of a service or policy and which therefore corresponds to concepts such as effectiveness, cost-effectiveness and 'value for money'.

The last of these terms, 'VFM', is a good example of the third problem related to the understanding and interpretation of the 3 'E's – the way different people make words and phrases mean what they want them to mean. This is particularly apparent when performance terminology has been used in political or managerial slogans and soundbites. In these cases the lack of precise meaning is advantageous and also allows their use as euphemisms. In the public sector the pursuit of VFM has often amounted to little more than the pursuit of greater economy.

The fourth reason relates to a lack of skills and experience in using even relatively simple quantitative data. Most people understand an indicator that is based on only one category of data – for example cost or volume – but there appears to be less comprehension of indicators that are ratios based on two categories of data – such as a unit cost which is a ratio of cost to output.

The Audit Commission's definition of effectiveness is also problematic because local authorities use the term in at least three ways:

- the extent to which targets/objectives are met;
- user satisfaction/assessment;
- 'technical' measures of the cause and effect that exists between service outputs on the one hand and outcomes on the other.

Despite the problems, the 3 'E's have remained the most frequently used way of defining performance. They are not however necessarily the foundation of performance information systems which are characterised by a mix of simple and ratio indicators. The most frequently used indicators can be categorised in terms of:

- cost
- volume of other resources – e.g. staff
- time targets/milestones
- service volume/outputs
- quality indicators such as speed of response, availability and user satisfaction
- service take-up
- capacity utilisation.

Equity and equality

Many local authorities were disappointed when the Citizen's Charter performance indicators initially contained no measures of equality, the Audit Commission having argued that it was not possible to produce such indicators. Notions of equity and equality are however of fundamental importance to local authorities in both their governmental and service delivery capacities, and in any case some authorities had already created their own indicators. Birmingham, for example, had developed a set of 12 indicators for equality, 6 relating to employment and 6 relating to service delivery. The concepts do however create problems of measurement because, like the 3 'E's, they can be used as slogans either lacking meaning or with different meanings. To be measured they have to be given precision so that appropriate data can be collected and comparisons made. Equality can be categorised in five ways so as to make it more amenable to measurement – equality of Expenditure; equality of Access; equality of Treatment; equality of Use; equality of Outcome.

Beyond the 'E's – an extended systems model of performance

The simple input-output-outcome model can be extended to incorporate more dimensions. One such approach is illustrated in Figure 5.1. In 'reading' the model the following issues need to be borne in mind.

- It is a systems model that remains based on the concept of inputs, process, outputs and outcomes. Like all such models it is an abstraction of reality and therefore has limitations.
- It attempts to emphasise the fundamental importance of incorporating information about and from the authority's environment, its citizens and its service users. This is represented in the top line of the model.
- It commences with an assumption that the specification of local political objectives, informed and supported by knowledge of the needs of the

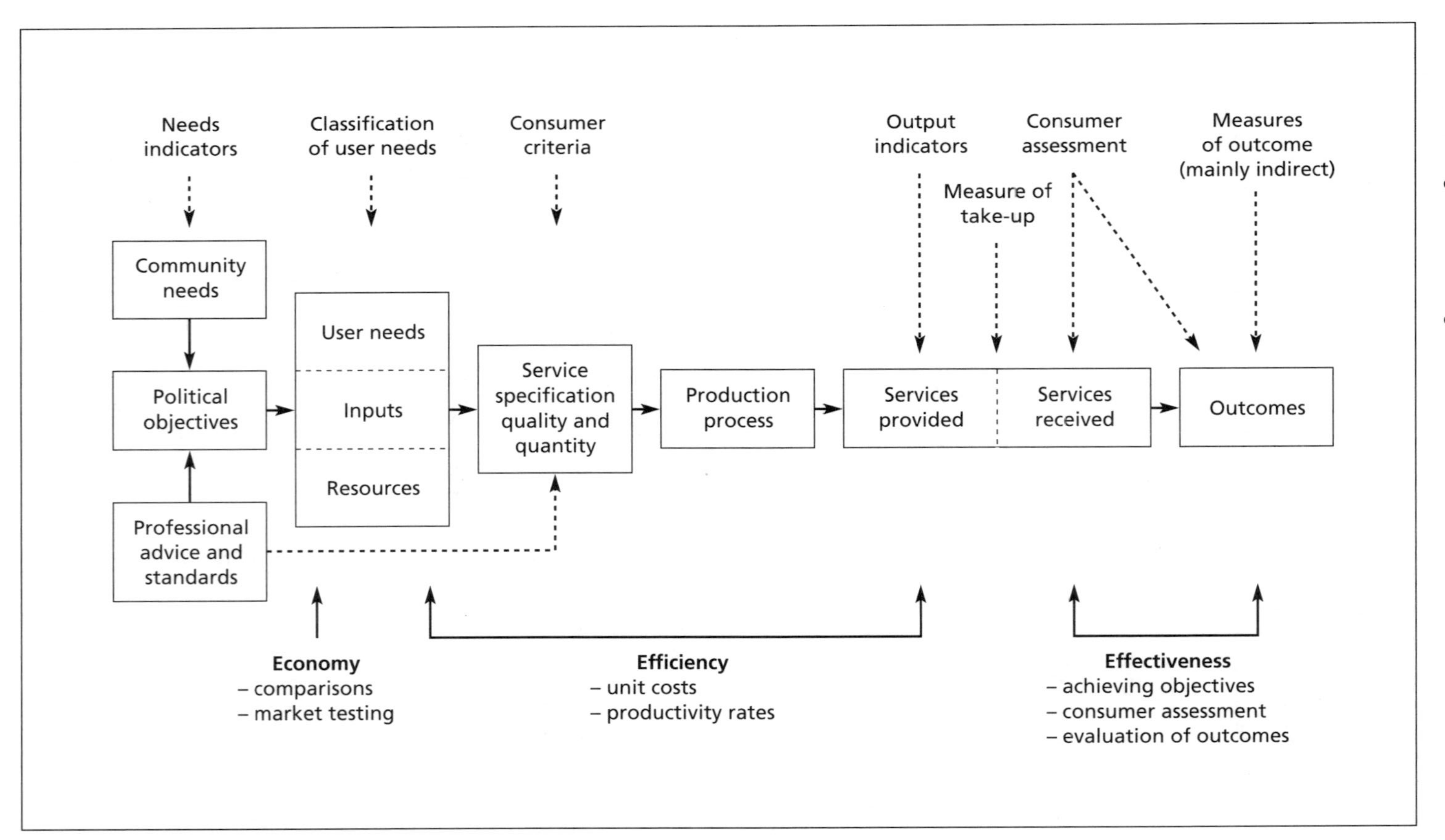

Figure 5.1 A model of performance management

community and by the advice of senior managers and professional staff, is the first step in specifying performance. It does not incorporate the fact that local objectives will also be informed (and sometimes dictated) by the policies, standards and targets of central government and its agencies.

- The model also incorporates the notion that, in systems terms, the needs of users and potential users are as much an input to the process as are the resources utilised. Children, for example, are an input to the education service which is designed in the light of their different education needs and expectations.
- The specification of services is an essential step in the process – for all services, not just those subjected to CCT or other forms of competition and contractualisation. If quality is an important dimension, then it is at this point that quality criteria have to be established and quality standards built into the service specification. It is also the point at which criteria of equity and equality should be specified.
- The double box – 'services provided and services received' – represents the fact that while the local authority views services as something which it produces, users see them as something they receive – and the two are always the same. Therefore services need to be viewed from both a production and a consumption viewpoint.
- Finally the model attempts to express the problem of 'effectiveness' by illustrating that it can be measured in the three ways specified above.

More complex models can be designed and for some purposes they are necessary. For example, for an organisation attempting to design its data systems from scratch and needing to understand all the data requirements of a comprehensive systems approach to performance, the kind of model represented in Figure 5.2 will be necessary. Miller's model of the data requirements emerging from a systems approach to performance measurement in the social services (Figure 5.2) results from a careful and comprehensive analysis of all the factors that are relevant to performance in that context. It is therefore essential for data system designers and should help managers and councillors understand the complexity of the 'system' they are attempting to guide and manage.

Developing a hierarchy of indicators

Developing a hierarchy of performance indicators can be helpful in clarifying what particular indicators are actually measuring and why and how they can be used. The following classification is one that may help local authorities in developing their indicators in relation to performance generally and for Best Value in particular:

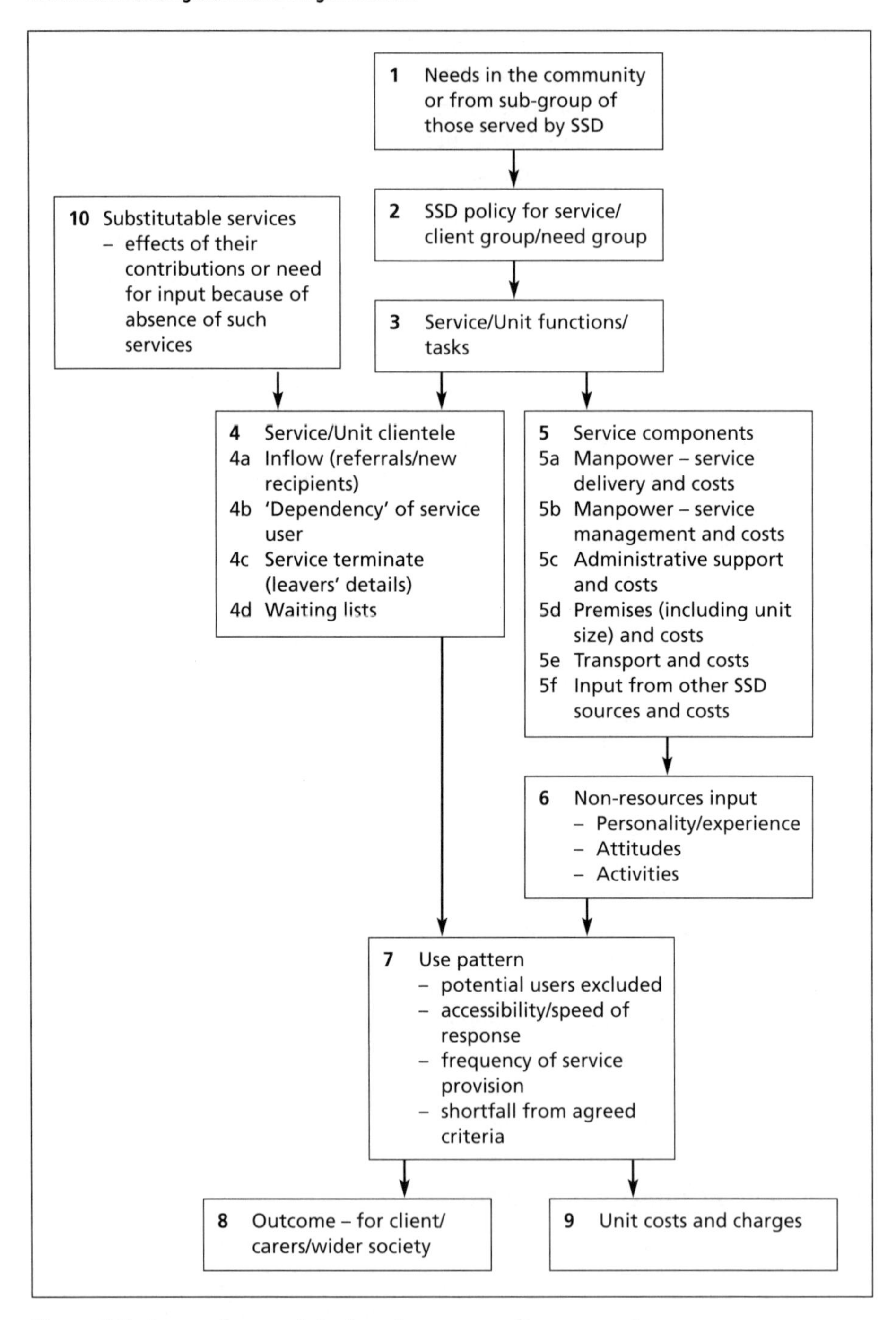

Figure 5.2 A complex model of performance measurement

Source: N. Miller: 'Management Information and Performance Measurement in the Personal Social Services' in Social Services Research: 1986 Nos 4 & 5 Dept of Social Admin, University of Birmingham

Level 1. Contextual indicators

(**A selection of key social, economic, environmental and demographic indicators**.)

These are not 'performance' indicators in the literal sense but nonetheless consist of the essential information that a local authority needs in order to:

— establish a baseline and trends in some of the core characteristics of its area;

— evaluate the impact of some of its policies and services;

— act as a basis and stimulus for policy review.

Level 2. Local democracy and governance

(**A selection of indicators that provide a basis for evaluating the extent and intensity of democratic behaviour and activity in the area**.)

This category of indicators is generally absent from existing sets of indicators but is nonetheless of fundamental importance in providing information about the 'health' of local democracy. In terms of precise measures it is an area which requires creative thinking and rigorous testing. Possible indicators are:

— the perceived effectiveness of communication;

— the perceived effectiveness of different modes of consultation;

— the perceived effectiveness of different modes of participation;

— satisfaction rates with the council and its services – categorised (as appropriate) by users, non-users, citizens, communities, visitors and also by area;

— electoral turnout;

— extent and variety of partnership arrangements;

— key financial indicators.

Level 3. Strategic priorities

(**A very small number of key performance indicators (KPIs) which enable councils to track and evaluate the implementation of their annually determined strategic priorities**.)

A number of councils already use the concept of 'KPIs' to help them track the policies they have identified as being of strategic importance. These indicators, which are necessarily specific to each priority, can be drawn from other levels in the hierarchy.

Level 4. Policy achievements and outcomes

(**Indicators relating to each of the council's main policies and/or objectives**.)

Indicators in this category need to relate primarily to the effectiveness and cost-effectiveness of corporate and service policies and, where appropriate, of nationally prescribed policies and targets. Because of the difficulty in measuring some areas of effectiveness it is likely that some indicators will be partial or proxy measures. They should, however, address the following specific areas:

— the extent of achievement of policy objectives and targets, whether they be stated in terms of outcomes, outputs or process;

— user/citizen evaluation of outcomes;

— where possible, the direct 'technical' measurement of the relationship between processes, outputs and outcomes.

Level 5. Service production and delivery

(**Indicators of service quality, volume, economy and efficiency, many of which can be compared with internal and external standards and benchmarks**.)

There are already extensive performance indicators in this area but further quality standards need to be developed for some services. Indicators in this category should include user assessment of the quality of service they receive.

Level 6. Organisational health

(**Indicators that assist in describing the organisation and relate to key organisational characteristics**.)

A considerable amount of descriptive data is recorded by many local authorities with regard to workforce profiles and costs, recruitment and exit data, and volume of training etc. – some of which is categorised by ethnicity, gender and disability. However, the data is not always brought together so that trends can be analysed and, when necessary, acted upon. Nor is this data always benchmarked against comparable organisations. Information on the health of the organisation and its staff is not so easily available, although there have been some developments (see, for example, Bramham, 1997). Some local authorities carry out occasional staff surveys, which can produce trend information but evidence from such surveys is limited and is rarely usable for comparative purposes. It is also possible that somewhat dubious proxy measures, such as the number of 'certificates' (i.e. ISO 9000, Investors in People, Charter Marks etc.) won and retained, might be developed.

By developing performance standards within a framework such as this one, it is likely that both councillors and officers can become more selective and more focused in their use of the mass of performance indicators which already exist and will no doubt continue to grow under the Best Value regime.

The Citizens Charter performance indicators

The most significant manifestation of the continuing drive to introduce greater control over local government and to make it more locally accountable was the introduction of the Citizens Charter initiative requirement to publish performance against a set of nationally determined performance indicators. The legislative basis for the specification and publication of performance indicators is contained in the Local Government Act (1992) which charged the Audit Commission with developing a set of performance indicators which could be used to make comparisons in terms of cost, economy, efficiency and effectiveness between different authorities and between different financial years. The Commission was authorised to give local authorities whatever directions it thought fit to achieve the legislative requirement.

The Audit Commission's approach

Faced with the daunting task of generating and implementing a set of performance indicators which would meet the government's explicit and implicit objectives whilst at the same time maintaining its relationships with local government, the Commission proceeded with both caution and speed. Extensive market surveys were undertaken to find out what citizens thought important about council services, what they understood by good performance, and what sort of information they would like published. The Commission then constructed a draft set of performance indicators on which it consulted local authorities and a wide range of other organisations. A final set of performance indicators, some 178 in all, was produced, together with advice and instructions on how the data was to be collected, the definition of each indicator and instructions for their publication locally.

The final determination of the specific indicators to be used in the first year suggested that the Commission had responded to some but not all of the comments it had received during its research and consultation exercises. It did, for example, simplify some indicators and also reduced the size of the total set. On the other hand, concern about the lack of indicators of quality was only addressed marginally and no attempt was made to include equality indicators.

The first year for collecting and publishing the performance indicators was 1993–94, with authorities being required to submit them to the Commission and to publish them by December 1994. In the early part of 1995 the Commission published its first annual reports based on a selection of the indicators which were presented in bar-chart form comparing the performance of authorities of a similar type. This approach has been repeated in subsequent years with some variation in reporting content and organisation, the most important of which has been that the Commission has incorporated year-on-year comparisons. The Commission has also published regular reports on the response to the publication of the performance indicators.

The Commission has attempted to adopt a role in relation to local authorities which is prescriptive, supportive and advisory. For example, 'Read All About It' (Audit Commission, 1994) contained extensive and generally helpful and well researched advice on how local authorities should go about publishing their indicators.

In publishing and commenting on the indicators, the Commission has gone to considerable lengths to present itself as operating as a neutral agent and carefully stated its aims with clarity and non-partisanship.

> *The Commission's aim is to stimulate an informed public debate about differences between councils in the standards of service they provide. The starting point for that debate is for the public to find out what some of those differences are, and that is the purpose of publishing this and the other volumes of indicators. (Audit Commission Vol. 2, 1995c)*

In reality, the Commission's role is inevitably prescriptive and judgmental:

- it specifies the total set of indicators and defines the individual indicators;
- it is able to choose which of the indicators it highlights in its annual reports;
- it is able to change the indicators from one year to another.

Public, political, professional and media reactions

The introduction and subsequent publication of local authority performance indicators has been accompanied by a vociferous debate. The Commission's own analysis, after the first year of operation, suggested that media coverage was 'substantial' at national and local levels and was also 'balanced in terms of its focus on both good and bad performance' (Audit Commission, 1995d). Research indicated that some 450 local newspapers and the majority of local radio and television stations covered the publication of the Commission's reports by highlighting the performance of local authorities in their own areas.

Analysis of Citizens Charter performance indicators

Despite the prominence and importance of the Citizens Charter performance indicators, there have been relatively few empirical analyses of the performance data. Boyne argues that this lack of analysis is significant, 'because an evaluation of performance indicators should not only identify their strengths and weaknesses in theory, but also attempt to apply and interpret them in practice' (Boyne, 1997).

The Audit Commission and local authorities need to be much clearer about what criteria or dimensions of performance the indicators are really measuring. Boyne's analysis concluded that almost a third of the performance indicators were crude financial measures which did not even provide information on economy. He comments:

> *The upshot of the conceptual and practical problems is that few of the Audit Commission indicators are useful for comparing the performance of local authorities. Only nineteen such indicators remain out of the total of two hundred and eighteen. A further six measures of performance can be derived by combining some of the indicators, or by combining single indicators with other variables such as population size. (Boyne, 1997)*

Boyne then takes his 20 remaining 'true' indicators of performance and places them in six categories: service coverage; service quality; service speed; service efficiency; service utilisation; and administrative effectiveness.

Lewis's analysis of the 178 indicators carried out during 1995-96 suggested the following categories:

Indicators giving **background information**	= 21% of total
Indicators of **performance**	= 37%
Indicators of **cost**	= 22%
Indicators of **quality**	= 20%
	100%

(Lewis, 1996)

While the Audit Commission does provide some commentary and analysis of the results when it publishes the annual performance indicators each March, the analysis is relatively brief and tends to be limited to comments about the performance achieved by local authorities as a whole or individually. There is little or no analysis of the performance indicators themselves.

Problems and pitfalls of performance measurement

Critics of performance measurement provide numerous arguments that suggest the need to use performance indicators with care. Stewart and Walsh (1995), for example, identify the following difficulties.

- No set of measures is complete and the validity of any measure can be disputed in the arena of public debate.
- The fact that performance in the public domain has many relevant dimensions creates the need for many measures.
- Complexity arises because of the interaction between the dimensions and measures of performance.
- Integrating different measures is difficult because of the different values that may be attached to them.

Smith (1993), writing in the context of the NHS, has helpfully identified seven distortional and dysfunctional effects of performance measurement, all of which are relevant to local government.

- **Tunnel vision** – caused by concentrating only on those aspects of performance which are measured – to the exclusion of other important aspects.
- **Sub-optimisation** – the pursuit by managers of their own narrow objectives, at the expense of strategic co-ordination.
- **Myopia** – concentration on short-term issues, to the exclusion of long-term criteria.
- **Convergence** – an emphasis on not being exposed as an outliner on any indicator rather than a desire to be outstanding.
- **Ossification** – a disinclination to experiment with new and innovative methods.
- **Gaming** – altering behaviour so as to obtain strategic advantage.
- **Misrepresentation** – including 'creative accounting and fraud.

  (Smith, 1993)

Requirements for the successful use of performance indicators

Several commentators have produced lists of principles for developing and using performance indicators. Jackson (1995), for example, proposes nine principles: consistency, comparability, clarity, controllability, comprehensiveness, contingency factors, limitation to key indices, relevance and feasibility. Likierman identifies the following '20 early lessons from managerial use' of performance indicators.

Concept

1 *Include all elements integral to what is being measured.*

2 *Choose a number appropriate to the organisation and its diversity.*

3 *Provide adequate safeguards for 'soft' indicators, particularly quality.*

4 *Take account of accountability and politics.*

Preparation

5 *Devise indicators with people on the ground, who must feel ownership.*

6 *Build in counters to short-term focus.*

7 *Ensure that indicators fairly reflect the efforts of managers.*

8 *Find a means to cope with uncontrollable items and perceived injustices.*

9 *Use the experience of other organisations or other parts of the organisation.*

10 *Establish realistic levels of attainment before the first targets are set.*

Implementation

11 *Recognise that new indicators need time to develop and may need revision in the light of experience.*

12 *Link them to existing systems.*

13 *They must be easily understandable by those whose performance is being measured.*

14 *While proxies may be necessary, they must be chosen cautiously.*

15 *The period of introduction should be used to reassess internal and external relationships.*

Use

16 *The data on which the results are based must be trusted.*

17 *Use the results as guidance, not answers. Recognise that interpretation is the key to action.*

18 *Acknowledge the importance of feedback. Follow-up gives credibility; no feedback means atrophy; negative-only feedback encourages game-playing.*

19 *Trade-offs and complex interactions must be recognised; not all indicators should carry equal weight.*

20 *Results must be user-friendly and at appropriate levels of aggregation and response time.*

(Likierman, 1993)

An analysis of lists such as these leads to the conclusion that three general categories of change are needed.

- Technical changes – which will enable more complex and quicker interrogation of data together with greater ability to produce a wider variety of reports.
- Conceptual changes – which are needed to develop a better theoretical understanding of the dimensions of performance.
- Cultural and attitudinal changes – which will lead to a greater use of performance information by a wider range of actors.

The future of performance measurement

Star ratings

Miller (1996) introduced his critique of the limitation of an accountancy approach to performance by producing an illuminating comparison with the star rating systems used for restaurants. Troman also proposes that an approach similar to hotel star, rosette or crown rating systems could be applied to local authority services. He suggests a star rating system to reflect the quality of physical facilities, the range of service provision and the quality of service but admits that 'the quality of service is more difficult to measure' (Troman, 1994).

The Charter Mark, Investors in People and ISO9000 initiatives can be regarded as embryonic star rating systems and they are increasingly popular amongst local authorities. The current government's proposals with regard to 'beacon' councils and services can also be regarded in the same light. The critical issue is to know what the motivational effects are on organisations which participate in schemes that are either voluntary or compulsory. Most of the evidence we have relates to voluntary schemes where it is clear that some organisations make a decision not to participate for a variety of economic reasons – particularly where they are serving a very local market in which there is little direct competition. Such systems also raise questions concerning the continuing validity of the criteria used for awarding stars.

Because of the difficulty of establishing performance criteria and measures which are sufficiently comprehensive, valid and reliable and also sufficiently discriminatory to be able to accurately assess performance at several levels, local government is not yet in a position to move to star rating systems.

Targets

The use of targets has become increasingly common and is practised by both central and local governments. Targets are applied most usually to the more simply measured aspects of performance such as speed of response. Some targets incorporate a level of performance as well as a time element, such as the target set by the government to achieve 25 per cent of all waste recycled by the year 2000. With more experience in the use of targets it may be anticipated that local and central government will become more skilled in identifying targets that are appropriate and relevant.

Standards and benchmarks

For the same reason that targeting has and will continue to increase then so will the use of standards. Whereas targets are something to aim for and therefore need to be used with the expectation that they will not necessarily be achieved, standards, particularly in the sense of minimum standards, are levels of performance which should be achieved. The centralisation of government in the UK has already led to the introduction of more standards and this is likely to continue. Benchmarking, which is already being developed by the Audit Commission and by local authority benchmarking clubs, is likely to be a favoured route for developing more national standards. It is noticeable that the concept of Best Value has already led to an increase in benchmarking activities by local authorities.

Performance measurement and Best Value

The government has indicated that performance indicators, both national and local, will form an essential part of the process for achieving Best Value. If the broader objectives of Best Value are to be achieved, in particular the concern for the democratic process and the 'value' provided by local authorities in general, then a new framework of performance indicators will be required which moves beyond the current use of simple input-output-outcome models used to produce the 3 'E's.

Although the development of Best Value is in its early stages at the time of writing, the evaluators of the English pilot projects at Warwick University have already produced their initial thoughts on such a framework for the pilot authorities to consider. This framework suggests that performance indicators will need to be developed within three tiers – core baseline data, service specific indicators, and local indicators. It is the first of these tiers which initially represents the most interesting development in that it proposes a twin focus on 'outcome' and on 'process'. In terms of outcome, there are proposals for core indicators in the following four areas:

- service quality
- cost-effectiveness
- community involvement in decision making
- contribution to democratic renewal.

In terms of process the four aspects are:

- efficiency of operation
- reliability and continuous quality improvement
- partnership working
- innovativeness and adaptiveness in service provision.

In each of these areas a number of illustrative performance indicators have been put forward for consideration, development and improvement by the pilot authorities. For example, with regard to community involvement the following indicators have been suggested:

- percentage of residents/users/businesses/community groups involved in participative activities;
- percentage of residents involved in any community activities related to BV services;
- percentage of residents/users/businesses/community groups making written comments on BV services per year;
- percentage of participants expressing satisfaction with participative opportunities in BV services;

(Warwick University – information supplied to Best Value pilot authorities, 1998).

These proposals, together with others that have been suggested, are open to questioning in terms of their appropriateness, validity and reliability, but they do open up new lines of thinking about the way in which local authority performance should be evaluated and measured. If, as the evaluators hopefully intend, they successfully provide a challenge to the pilot authorities to develop better indicators within the proposed framework, then they are likely to prove the source of some necessarily creative thinking in this difficult and contentious area.

Questions

1 *Consider the following statements and decide to **what** extent you in general agree or disagree with them, **why** you agree or disagree with them – and identify whether there are any circumstances that might cause you to change your views.*

- *If you can't measure it you can't manage it.*
- *What gets measured gets done.*
- *If you can't measure results you cannot tell success from failure.*
- *If you can't measure success you cannot reward it.*
- *If you can't demonstrate success you cannot win public support.*
- *If you can't specify failure you cannot correct it.*
- *If you can't specify success and failure you cannot learn from them.*

2 *Collect together all the performance indicators and standards that are used to measure the performance of your service and try to determine the **criteria** of performance on which they are based. Are there any criteria that you believe are important for evaluating your service that are not included? If so, can you explain why they have not been included? Finally, identify some indicators or standards that do measure the missing criteria.*

3 *Now think about the way in which those indicators are actually used in your authority. Who uses them? When are they used? What are they used for and what kinds of decisions are they used to inform? If you find that some of the indicators do not get used at all, can you explain why this should be so?*

4 *Return to Chapter 3 and reread the part which provides some criteria for evaluating the concept of Best Value. To what extent has your local authority developed indicators or standards in relation to any of the criteria mentioned?*

6

Managing organisational performance

Introduction

In the first edition of this book three categories of performance management systems were identified. In the intervening eight years it has no longer become possible to identify different categories as clearly because most local authorities are now responding to the same kind of pressures with similar concepts and models. In so far as differences exist they are more a matter of the precise balance each achieves in attempting to accommodate and reflect the variety of objectives that are built into the basic concept of performance management.

They do however differ in the extent to which corporate systems have a real impact on the everyday decisions and activities of the local authority, with some clearly having a great impact, acting as they are intended to do, as a core organisational process for steering the authority. Others, having become bureaucratised and sidelined, have become paper-generating exercises with less relevance to the real life of the authority.

In this chapter, a number of themes will be identified that are currently of importance in understanding the way performance management is developing; then examples will be explored in order to provide some understanding of the way in which individual authorities are using performance management. Finally, there will be an analysis of some of the issues and circumstances which appear to help determine whether performance management is a mainstream, 'on-line' management process or not.

Driving forces for performance management

Five driving forces may be identified that have led to the introduction of performance management in recent years.

- **The search for strategy and a sense of direction and purpose** – accepting the general criticism that local government lacked a sufficient sense of strategic direction and sensing that the reductions in the powers of local government had obscured its fundamental democratic role and purpose, a number of local authorities have implemented a more strategic approach. This typically includes the development of mission statements, corporate strategies and policies and at least an attempt at longer-term and more integrated financial, human resource and facilities planning. In some authorities these developments were seen as separate from performance management while in others they were regarded as integral.
- **Accountability** – apart from having to respond to the government's legislative requirements, local authorities have been proactive in developing their own mechanisms for accountability. The use of service contracts, citizens contracts, local citizens charters and a variety of forms of public consultation and participation are all examples of their preparedness to move beyond the legislative requirements. The search for internal accountability has also been a major stimulus for the introduction of performance management.
- **Achievement – the quest for quality** – under pressure to achieve greater economy and efficiency, local authorities introduced a variety of performance review mechanisms which had varying degrees of success. The focus on economy and efficiency – at the expense of effectiveness and quality – led to increasing expressions of concern within local authorities some of whom began to introduce ideas drawn from the Quality Management movement. As a consequence, there was an increasing shift during the late 1980s and early 1990s towards concepts of quality control, quality assurance and even Total Quality Management. In some cases the concern for quality was integrated within a performance management framework, while in other cases the two approaches appeared to be pursued independently. In some authorities the language of 'performance management' was largely abandoned in favour of that of 'quality management'.
- **Survival** – the requirements to compete for customers (through the legislation extending the area of customer choice) and for work (through the mechanism of CCT) have forced local authorities to review the volume and range of services they provide. Economy and efficiency have

been pursued as a necessity for survival rather than as a model of good management.

- **Learning** – the inclusion of a capacity to learn as a central part of the definition of performance management presented in Chapter 1 has in practice been achieved in few local authorities. It has, however, been assisted by the increased attention given to organisational learning as a condition of corporate development and survival in the private sector and to its promulgation by management gurus such as Peter Senge (1993). The need to be creative and flexible in responding to changing community needs and to the vagaries of the government grant system has led more local authorities to recognise that the organisational and individual capacity to learn from past successes and failures and the ability to learn how to utilise new ideas and methods has become a core requirement of life in local government.

An emerging, standardised performance management process?

Figure 6.1 illustrates what appears to be a commonly accepted, 'standardised' model of performance management in local government. The key aspects of the model are as follows.

Analysis and review of the external environment

The model illustrates the increasing attempts by local authorities to carry out a systematic review of the external environment as the starting point for the process. The 'environment' in this case consists of three elements.

- Local socio-economic, demographic, employment, economic activity and physical trends – monitored by means of a set of key indicators – collected through regular opinion surveys, other market research methods and direct feedback from citizens and service users.
- Analysis of the local implications of new UK and European legislation (actual and anticipated), new rules, regulations, statutory instruments and directives, and a consideration of actual and anticipated changes in government political philosophy and direction.
- Consideration of the local majority party's own changing political philosophy and direction.

An emerging fourth element – consideration of the plans and activities of other major public service provision organisations – can be identified in some local

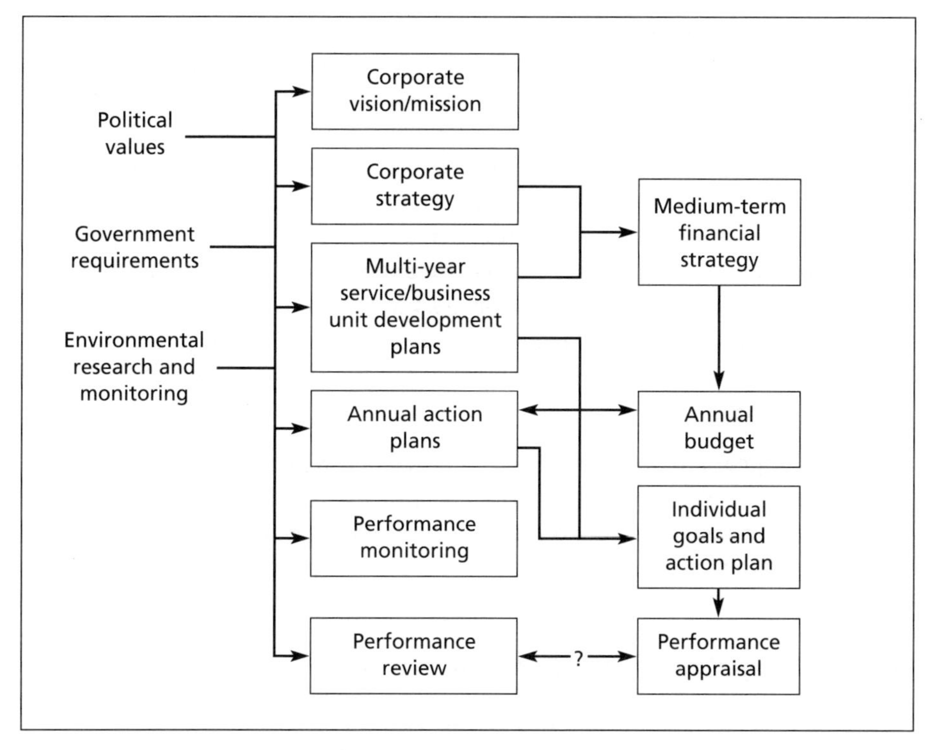

Figure 6.1 A typical corporate strategic and peformance management process

authorities but is not yet fully integrated in most local authorities. This aspect of performance management is discussed below as one of the thematic issues.

Integration of strategy and implementation

The process identified in Figure 6.1 exemplifies the attempt to ensure that there is a clear link between the specification of strategy and its practical application in service delivery. The development of 'Action Planning', which has become de rigueur in most local authorities, represents a distinct shift in management style in local government in recent years. Today it is difficult to find a local authority that does not have action plans – or their equivalent in the shape of business or service development plans.

Integration of strategy and service plans with the budgetary process

Many local authorities have made repeated attempts to achieve better integration of the annual budgetary process with the strategy formulation and service planning process but in reality the link often remains a weak one. This is due, in part, to the lateness of the government's public spending and grant allocation announcements each year, making it difficult for local authorities to formulate their plans before then. But it is also apparent that there is a reluctance in some local authorities to undertake any forward financial planning until they have a precise and full knowledge of the resources available to them in the following year. This predisposition is an unrealistic one, based on an assumption that planning can only be achieved once full information about the future is available. Full information can never be available and all planning has to take place in the midst of degrees of uncertainty. Numerous local authorities have demonstrated, by introducing a three or four year medium-term financial strategy, that full and precise knowledge of future resources is not a prerequisite to forward financial planning.

There also appears to be, in some local authorities, a problem relating to the 'ownership' of the strategic and budgetary processes, with Treasurers and Finance Committees retaining quasi-independent control of the latter. As a consequence, there is a failure to relate the separate processes of policy or strategy development to those of service development and delivery.

Integration of organisational and individual performance

Figure 6.1 illustrates the way that some local authorities have sought to ensure that the process for setting goals and action plans for individuals is related to the process for planning organisational performance. The linkage is often not a perfect one, there being recurring problems with the timing of the process and the conceptual and practical problems of cascading goals and objectives to all levels of the organisation, but many local authorities appear to have made considerable improvements in the way they do this. These are explored in Chapter 7.

Building in monitoring and review

Figure 6.1 also illustrates the fact that local authorities have recognised the importance of ensuring that the monitoring and review of organisational and individual performance is built into the annual process for managing performance. The extent to which this is achieved in practice appears to vary considerably from one local authority to another and there continues to be a problem (represented by the question mark in Figure 6.1) in creating an effective link between the review of individual performance and the review of service and corporate performance. Best Value has created the need to develop a more extensive, more fundamental and integrated approach to the review of organisational performance.

Models of performance management such as that contained in Figure 6.1 are now commonplace and later in this chapter examples of how individual local authorities have interpreted and implemented the model will be explored. Such models can be dangerous because they can hide as much as they reveal. They are, at best, illustrations of how a local authority intends to manage performance or how it thinks it ought to manage performance. They are not necessarily descriptions of how it does so in practice. Such models describe only the formal organisational processes and systems. They contain no reference to other characteristics of organisational life that are fundamental to the way that performance is really managed, such as organisational and political culture and expectations and the information systems, both 'soft' and 'hard', that are needed to underpin the process.

Performance management systems in local authorities

The late 1980s

The three categories of performance management systems identified in the first edition of this book were as follows.

- **Group 1 systems: the business approach** – these approaches focused exclusively on the management of organisational performance, were very much 'business' oriented and were clearly a response to the Thatcher Government's drive for greater economy, efficiency and, to a lesser extent, effectiveness. The examples provided were Arun District Council's Corporate Business System (Arun, 1987) and the first phase of the development of the London Borough of Bexley's Business Process (Burgess, 1983 and Bexley, 1989). A third example, Chesterfield Borough Council's Corporate Planning System (Chesterfield, 1989), adapted earlier developments in corporate planning to provide a more business oriented focus.
- **Group 2 systems: the integration of organisational and individual performance** – these systems were examples of explicit and systematic attempts to drive down through the organisation to the individual employee level the processes of planning, monitoring, reviewing and improving performance. They represented, in differing degrees, an attempt to integrate bottom-up with top-down performance management. The examples given were the second phase of the London Borough of Bexley's Business Process, Cambridgeshire County Council's corporate, service and individual planning and review process and the Royal Borough of Windsor and Maidenhead's Performance Management Programme.

- **Group 3 systems: the contracting authority** – this grouping, represented by authorities such as Lincolnshire County Council, was developing an internal contract culture as the core driving force behind the way each authority was managed, with extensive use of internal contracts and service level agreements. They were not only a response to the implications of CCT but were an acceptance of the principle that 'contracts' and 'a contract culture' were to become the basic building blocks for managing organisations.

Performance management systems today

An examination of performance management in those authorities that have identifiable and clear systems today suggests that they have been influenced by the following ideas.

- The use of internal contracting as a mechanism for managing performance. Contracts exist both at the organisational level (i.e. between units or departments within the authority) and the individual level (at least for senior managers). Experience with the use of internal contracting has been variable and some authorities have been through a learning curve which has involved first the development of detailed contracts, then the realisation that such contracts do not necessarily lead to improvements in performance and create other problems such as an unnecessary and inappropriate degree of internal competition and conflict. This has led, finally, to a more limited and discrete use of relational forms of contracting that focus in a more balanced way on the maintenance of appropriate relationships within the authority.
- The integration of concepts of quality management into performance management has been achieved in a number of ways. Work with 'quality circles' has led to the more extensive involvement of front-line and other junior staff in identifying ways of improving performance. It has also influenced the development of mechanisms for ensuring that there is a better bottom-up flow of feedback from front-line staff to senior management – although in practice the extent to which this has been successful remains limited. The use of the Business Excellence Model (see pp. 58–9) is also an example of the way quality has influenced performance.
- The more extensive use of performance measures and targets. The philosophy of targeting appears to be commonplace and while local authorities appear to be giving more attention to performance measurement there remain some local authorities that make little practical use of such measures. Nonetheless the performance and service plans of most local authorities do reflect a general change in this area. Whereas the

column in such plans labelled 'performance measures' or 'performance targets' was often blank or only sketchily completed, most plans today have fuller, more relevant and carefully considered entries.

- The use of business planning concepts. Although the term 'business planning' is used in different ways in local government, its influence can be seen in a number of ways: the identification of 'business' or 'service' units as a focal point for service planning and performance management; the greater specification of business and service objectives and targets for each unit; and the use of a variety of concepts associated with business planning such as SWOT analysis. In some authorities the creation of business units has led to the greater internal fragmentation of the authority as units have been encouraged or allowed to compete with each other and pursue their own business goals rather than the goals of the authority as a whole.
- The introduction of concepts of strategic planning and management which have also had a strong influence on the way that performance management systems have developed. Combined with continuing financial pressure and a growing political culture of specifying a few key targets and 'pledges', the practice of determining key corporate and service priorities and targets has become increasingly commonplace.

The Audit Commission's approach

The Audit Commission's model of performance management contains six 'functions'.

- **Specification of objectives** – specific questions are posed concerning the existence of mission and core values, the existence of corporate aims and their translation down through the organisation in the form of objectives and targets and action plans, and the existence of corporate strategic planning, monitoring and review systems.
- **Financial/Business planning** – the relationship of the budget process to business and action planning.
- **Performance review** – the arrangements for monitoring, measuring, reviewing and improving performance.
- **Individual appraisal**.
- **External communication** – the requirements for external reporting and communication, responsiveness to external views and needs, the use of external comparisons and best practice, and arrangements for public complaints.
- **Internal communication** – the need for effective internal communication of policies and practice. (Audit Commission, 1995b)

Having provided local government with the 3 'E's, it was not altogether surprising that the Commission should have invented the 10 'C's as a description of the steps necessary for the successful implementation of performance management. Divided into three groups, each of which represented the Commission's views of the main stages for implementation, they were as follows.

- *Making it real* – to ensure that objectives and priorities are realistic and meaningful three steps are necessary.
  1. **Consultation** – on objectives and priorities in order to build staff ownership.
  2. **Clarification** – by establishing objectives and key tasks at every level of the organisation.
  3. **Credibility** – by ensuring that objectives are realistic, measurable and can be operationalised.
- *Making it happen* – organising the authority to ensure that objectives are delivered by taking four steps.
  4. **Commitment** – sustaining councillor and chief officer commitment and developing champions further down the organisation.
  5. **Continuity** – following through and improving processes for long-term change.
  6. **Communication** – continuous communication, linked to training, to ensure staff understanding.
  7. **Conflict** – identify and resolve conflicts to enable progress to be made.
- *Making it work* – ensuring that staff are able to perform and that performance is monitored and improved by taking three steps.
  8. **Competence** – train staff in new approach and the responsibilities that arise from it.
  9. **Control** – develop systems for control and accountability that are not bureaucratic.
  10. **Consolidation** – monitor and review in order to improve performance and the operation of the process. (Audit Commission, 1995b)

The Audit Commission's handbook on performance management contained ten case studies of performance management, each one representing a particular aspect of performance management. They were:

- Cambridgeshire County Council – 'an example of an integrated PM system developed with the assistance of management consultants';

- Royal Borough of Windsor and Maidenhead – 'an example of an integrated PM system';
- Berkshire County Council – 'an example of using business planning to support contract management';
- Fareham Borough Council – 'an example of using PM to change organisational culture';
- Hampshire County Council – 'an example of an integrated PM system used to maintain control and accountability in a devolved management structure';
- Lewisham Borough Council – 'an example of a personal appraisal scheme';
- Nottinghamshire County Council – 'an example of developing and communicating a single vision';
- Redditch Borough Council – 'an example of performance review';
- Solihull Metropolitan Borough Council – 'an example of an integrated PM system focused on customer service';
- Swale District Council – 'an example of an integrated PM system focused on organisational improvement'. (Audit Commission, 1995b)

Examples of local authority approaches to performance management systems

The following examples have been selected not because they can with certitude be described as 'best practice' – indeed to imply that there is one best way would be inappropriate – but because they all contain aspects of good practice and reflect different ways in which local authorities have designed systems and procedures for managing performance.

St Edmundsbury Borough Council (see Figure 6.2)

The diagram of St Edmundsbury's Corporate Planning Process is a typical example of those local authorities that have in recent years developed an integrated system for managing performance that brings together all the main elements in a carefully ordered and timed annual process. The process is set within a context of considerable change as the council seeks not only to manage its own services as well as possible but also to develop a community leadership and partnership role with a variety of local organisations. The process has been developed in order to achieve a number of objectives.

- To ensure that changes to service provision only occur when they support the council's overall aims and objectives.

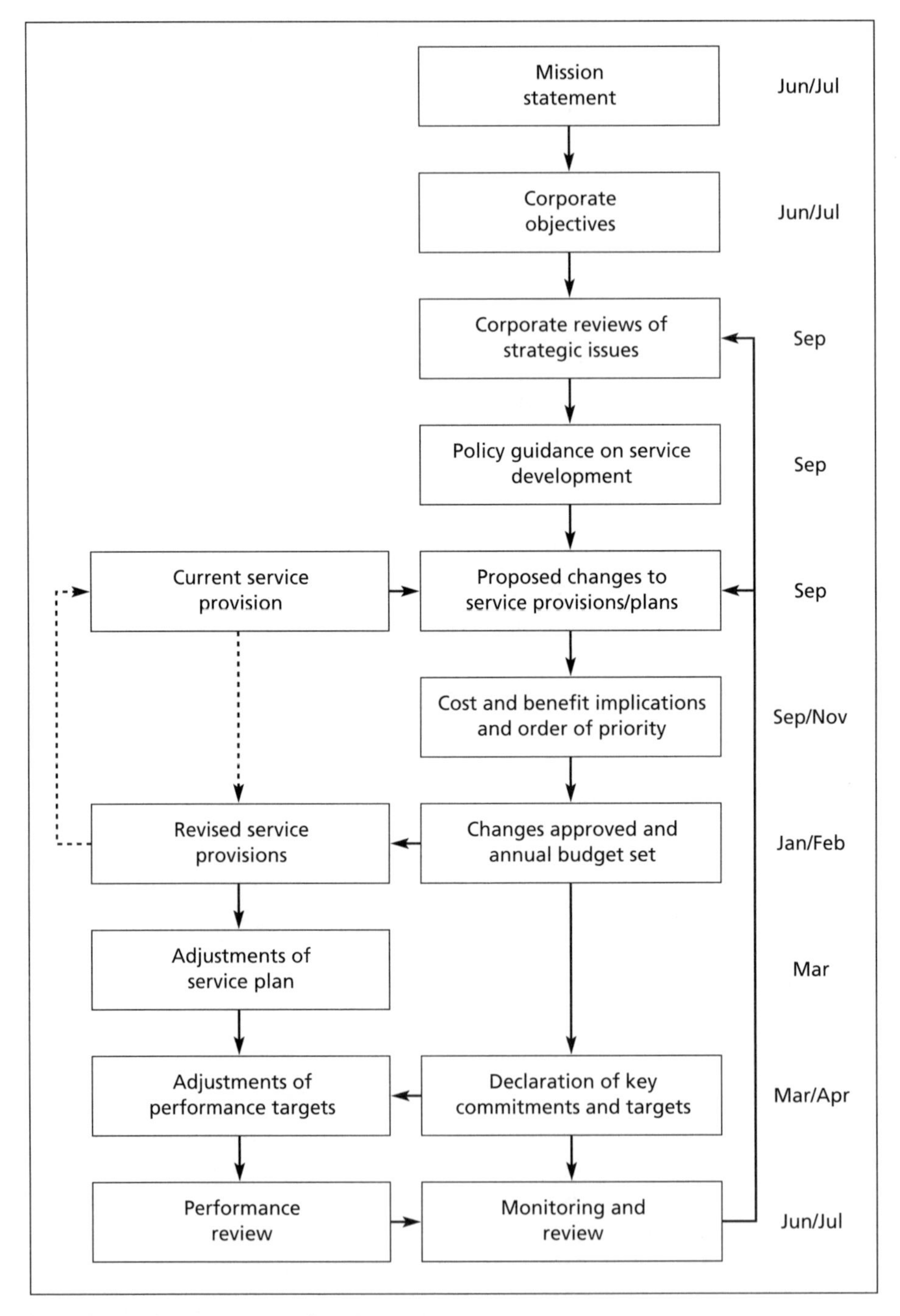

Figure 6.2 The corporate planning process

Source: St Edmundsbury Borough Council – Extending Excellence by Working with Communities: Corporate Plan, 1995–99

- To ensure that the costs and benefits of each proposal for change are fully considered (a common format for all change proposals has been designed to help achieve this).
- To ensure that change proposals can be given a corporate priority ranking that can be used as the basis for allocating resources to them.
- To ensure that service plans, which are seen as a statement of commitment by the council, incorporate agreed service changes.
- To ensure that performance targets for sections and individuals are realistically adjusted in the light of the agreed changes.
- To help enable the council, to publish with confidence and clarity an annual statement of key commitments and targets.
- To ensure that monitoring and review is built in as an integral part of political and managerial decision making. This is done in three ways: management review – which focuses on both organisational and individual performance; members' review – using regular reporting on progress and performance; and public review – which allows the public to express their views on the council's performance on the basis of the information provided in an annual report. (St Edmundsbury B.C., 1996)

Apart from being a well-developed system, the approach in St Edmundsbury is one which ensures a fairly high degree of central control. It is an approach which is not uncommon in those shire district councils that have fully developed performance management systems but is found less frequently in larger multi-purpose authorities. The council has also agreed a set of ten 'corporate objectives'. These are statements about how the council and its staff intend to behave rather than a set of substantive policy statements. The latter are expressed in a detailed set of 'key commitments' and in a 'community action plan'. The corporate objectives include statements on such things as: the setting and publishing of quality standards; reviewing and improving performance; developing a committed workforce to serve the community; and prudent financial planning and clear budgetary controls.

Cambridgeshire County Council (see Figure 6.3)

Cambridgeshire provides a very good example of a local authority that was one of the early leaders in local government in developing an integrated performance management system but which, unlike some other authorities, has constantly sought to improve its approach. The strength of the Cambridgeshire approach lies in the way it links the processes for managing organisational performance to the individual. The organisational process consists of an overall vision that is translated into strategic policies, priorities and plans. These are the basis for the business and service plans that are in

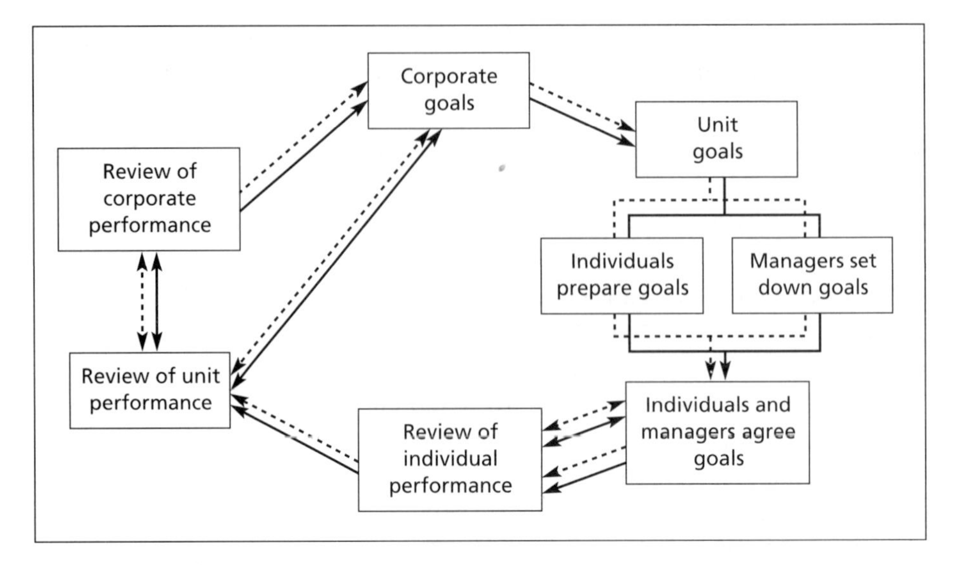

Figure 6.3 Performance management
Source: Cambridgeshire County Council

turn the basis for determining departmental, divisional and section objectives. These provide the context within which a highly developed process of individual performance management is carried out. This process involves the specification of individual accountabilities, performance measures and standards, goals and action plans that are monitored by means of regular progress reviews and annual performance reviews. Although the system for managing individual performance has remained basically the same over a number of years, it has been supplemented and improved by giving more emphasis to training and the development of a learning culture, the use of competencies, and the introduction of 360° review.

The London Borough of Bromley (see Figure 6.4)

Bromley's 12 box model was produced in 1993 in a discussion document, as a summary of the planning and review process it considered was appropriate to achieve its aim of becoming an 'enabling' authority. Although produced four years before the Labour Party's success in the 1997 General Election, some of its language has a very contemporary ring to it:

> *In Bromley we accept the need to look for* **best value** *and use or work in* **partnership** *with the private and voluntary sectors where this is more cost effective. However, we also recognise the wider remit of an 'enabling' authority. Working within the law the Council should be the* **community leader***, promoting the well being of local communities which make up our Borough. (Bromley, 1993) (Author's emphasis)*

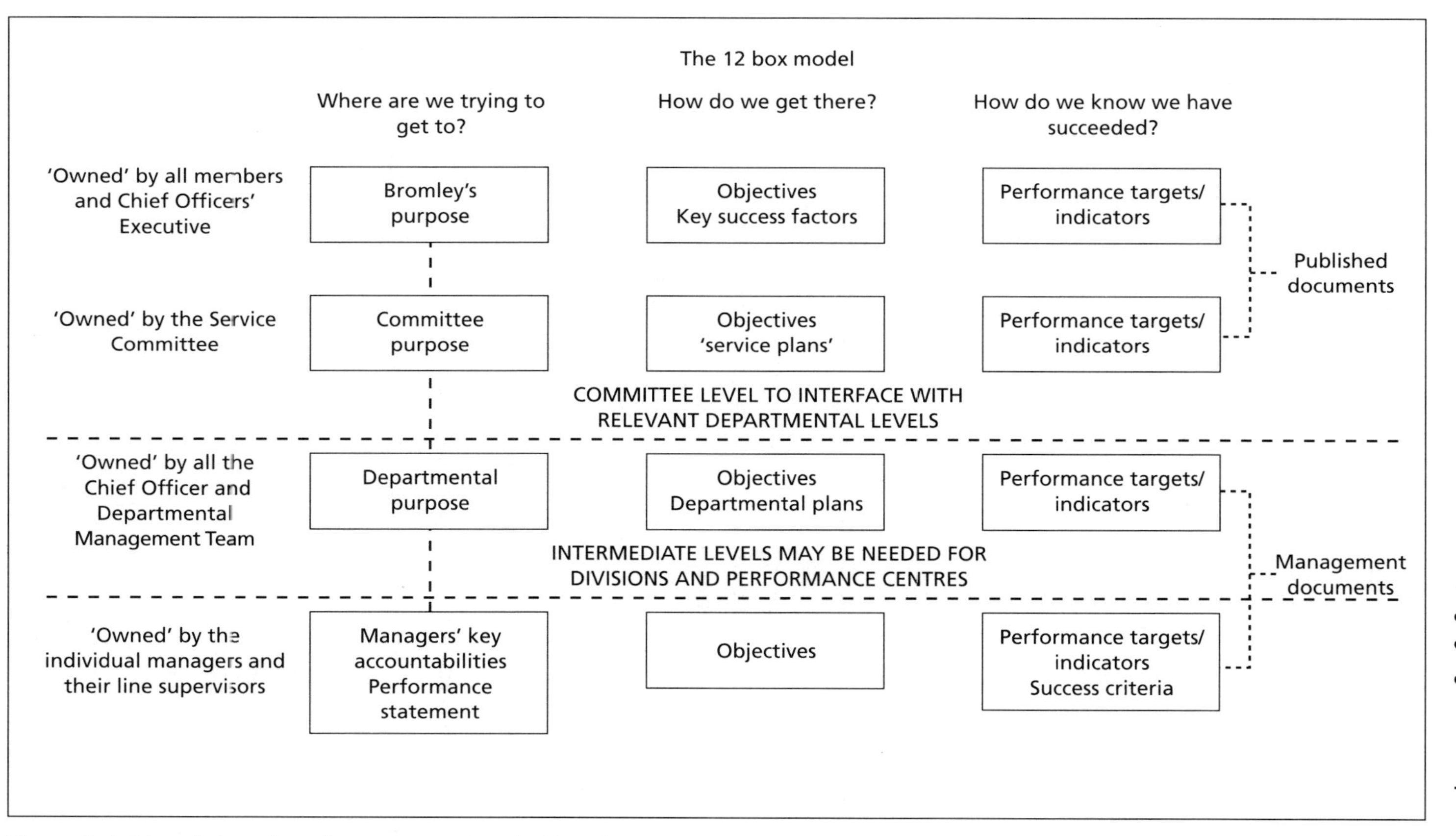

Figure 6.4 Planning and performance review in Bromley

Source: London Borough of Bromley – Responding to Change: Serving the People even Better, 1993

The model focuses on three main questions and shows how they relate to four levels in the organisation. The first of the questions, 'What are we trying to achieve?', is concerned with the establishment of purpose and aims. Corporate purpose and aims were identified and were to be put into practice by means of three management processes.

- *Management style* – 'the way we do things' – which was concerned with finding 'the right balance between stability, innovation and reorganisation'.
- *Employment style* – 'the values we put on our staff' – which was intended as a framework for personnel policies covering six issues: communication; remuneration; reorganisation; redundancy; a healthy workforce; and training and development.
- *Business style* – 'the systems we use' – which incorporated two elements, the design of the future organisation in terms of client, contractor and corporate centre roles, and the planning and performance review systems as illustrated by the model.

The second question, 'How do we get there?' relates to the setting of specific objectives within plans at each of the four levels of the organisation. The third question, 'How do we know we have succeeded?' relates to the monitoring and review of performance, using targets and indicators relevant to each level of the organisation.

Bromley's description of its system is particularly significant because it recognises that systems alone are insufficient. The concept of 'Management style – the way we do things' is an explicit acknowledgement of the importance of developing an organisational culture that matches the broad aims of the organisation and the systems by which it is managed.

Bolton Metropolitan Borough Council (see Figure 6.5)

Bolton's concept of 'Total performance management' was introduced in the early 1990s and gradually developed and clarified in subsequent years. Like several other metropolitan boroughs the process tends to be dependent on an extensive range of documentation. The model is applied to three levels of the organisation, corporate, departmental and unit. Figure 6.5 illustrates the model from the departmental perspective.

The *context* segment at the corporate level involves scanning the external environment and developing appropriate corporate strategic planning and resource allocation processes, policy guidance and strategies for managing and developing the organisation. The *strategic performance* segment is concerned with the long-term aims, objectives and policies of the council and

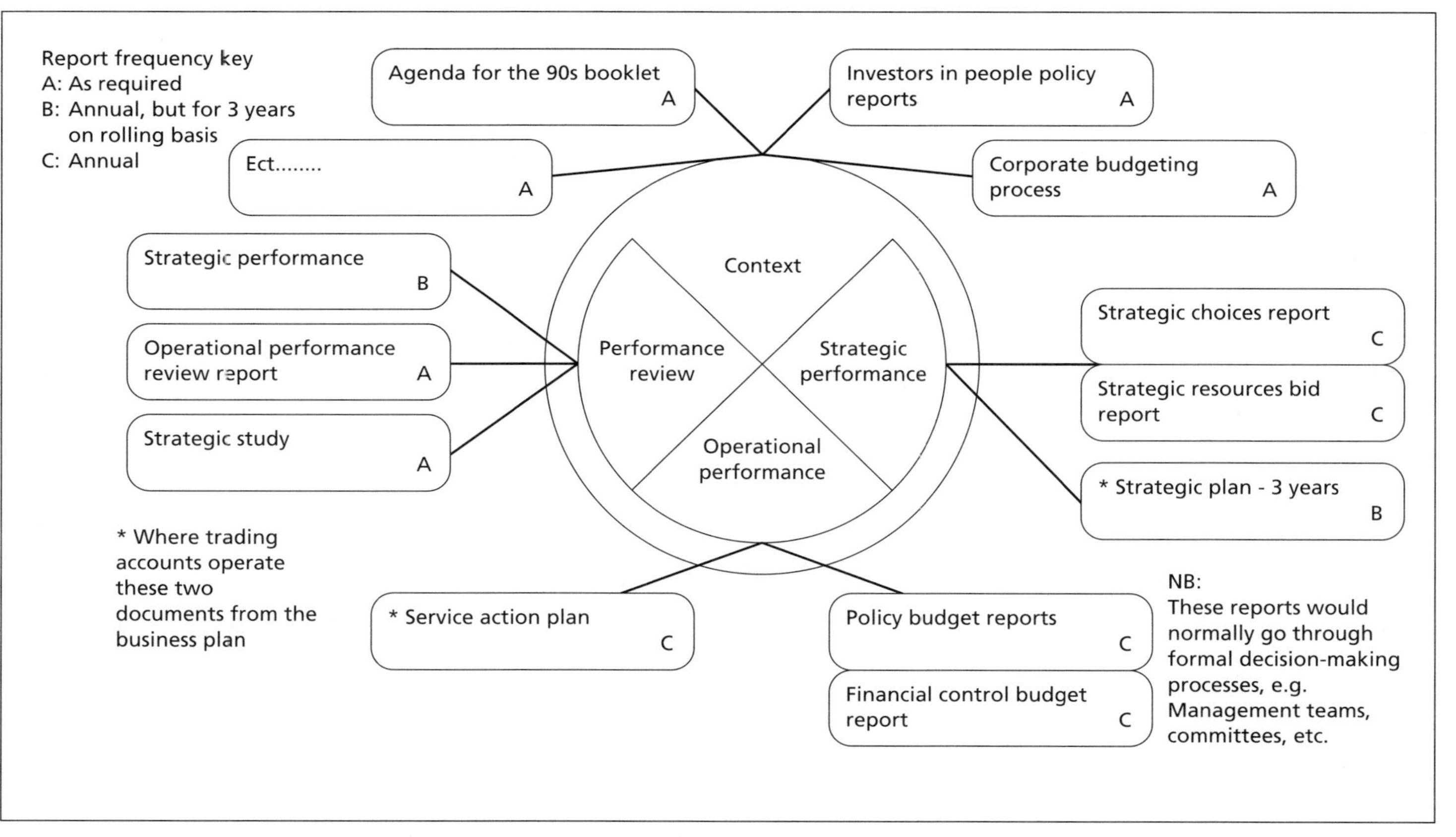

Figure 6.5 Total performance management and associated documentation
Source: Bolton Metropolitan Borough Council

involves a series of processes including: the identification of major issues and goals by committees; strategic review working parties to examine specific issues; the identification of priorities; and the formulation of strategic plans and budgets by each committee.

The *operational performance* segment is concerned with 'translating the thinking and planning into annual action and achievement' and is based on a service action planning process (or business planning process in trading departments). Although an outline process for action planning has been specified, this can be adapted by each department.

The final segment, *performance review*, completes one cycle and begins the next. It consists of four mechanisms: an annual strategic performance review of departments; operational performance monitoring and review as an ongoing process; and occasional strategic studies as required.

Bolton's representation of its approach conforms to a 'classical' approach to performance management and tends to produce a great deal of documentation. It is, however, an approach which reflects the need to develop processes at different levels of the organisation, that allow sufficient flexibility for the lower levels to be able to manage their services effectively, whilst at the same time retaining sufficient organisational unity.

Externally generated frameworks for managing performance

A number of local authorities have begun to use national and international frameworks as a basis for managing performance or as a supplement to their existing processes. 'Investors In People' (IIP) is one of the more popular frameworks with many local authorities applying for certification on either a corporate or service basis. However, although it has had a major impact in some authorities in encouraging a greater focus on individual appraisal, training and organisational development, it does not appear to have had a wider influence on performance management processes. Of greater relevance to the management of organisational performance has been the use of the Business Excellence Model of the European Foundation for Quality Management (EFQM) outlined in Chapter 4 (see Figure 4.1).

The Business Excellence Model has been used in different ways by different authorities. In the London Borough of Southwark it is being used as the basis of their overall framework for organisational management – 'Towards Service Excellence' – a total quality approach to the management of all its activities.

Having embarked on a number of initiatives such as Quality Assurance (ISO9000), IIP, business planning and benchmarking from 1995 onwards, the council identified the need to put these and other initiatives into a single strategic framework.

Cheshire County Council Social Services Department has also used the model, following its successful piloting in parts of the department during 1995, as a framework for strategic planning and management. The model was introduced at workshops where all senior and middle managers were involved in an assessment exercise followed by the identification of priorities for improvement and action plans. Further assessment exercises were carried out and a number of groups were set up using the EFQM model to examine the future of different areas of social services policy and activity. The model was also used to help the department prepare for local government reorganisation in 1998 and resulted in three specific developments: the development of a 'Continuous Improvement Plan' for the department; the development of a better link between improvement activity and the business planning process; and the identification of strategic objectives.

A surprisingly large proportion of the Best Value pilot bids were wholly or partly based on the EFQM model and several of these have been selected as pilot authorities. Solihull Metropolitan Borough Council, for example, having had a long history of developing its own systems for managing organisational and individual performance, has based its bid on the EFQM model as an integrating and holistic framework. Other authorities have developed their own frameworks that are partly derived from external models such as EFQM. Warwickshire County Council's Treasurer's Department, for example, developed a Quality Improvement Scheme which was subsequently sold to other authorities through CIPFA and is now being extended to all other departments as a central feature of the county council's Best Value pilot project.

The use of such externally generated models or frameworks is becoming increasingly popular and the evidence of their benefits in the private sector is clear. The EFQM model, for example, appears to be comprehensive. It has been adapted to the particular circumstances of local government and can be further adapted by individual authorities. It is comprehensible to both councillors and staff and can be used in a variety of ways. The danger of becoming dependent on such a model is that it may not, over time, prove to be as comprehensive and objective as it is now assumed. It also requires considerable initial investment, whereas the full benefits are only likely to accrue over an extensive period of time, and therefore needs to be seen as a long-term initiative which requires continuing further investment. The history of local government suggests that such management models, systems and 'solutions' can become associated with party political control and do not always, as a result, survive a change of political control.

Involving external stakeholders in strategic planning and performance management.

The increasingly dominant themes of community leadership, partnership and democratic renewal have resulted in some of the most interesting changes in the way local authorities are designing their processes for formulating strategies and specifying performance. The developments are all concerned with finding new and/or improved ways of involving groups of stakeholders who are external to the local authority, whether they be service users, individual citizens or partner organisations in the public, private or voluntary sectors. At present, the developments are variable and may not yet be sufficiently well integrated with existing internal systems but they nonetheless represent a significant development. Characteristically they involve the following kinds of processes.

- **Developing, with partner organisations, shared or joint strategies for the local community** – this development lies at the heart of the SOLACE concept of 'community planning' and Rogers' 'community strategy' model of community planning (Rogers and SOLACE, 1998). Local authorities have not yet achieved the development of shared corporate strategies with a range of other organisations but this has been done with a single organisation, for example with the health authority, or in relation to a single issue, client group or service area. Bury is one of several local authorities that have developed joint strategies for a client group or a specific segment of the population. Warwickshire County Council is one of a number of authorities that has developed area based partnership planning and/or action teams with other tiers of local government, health authorities, police, voluntary organisations, TECs etc.
- **Involving external stakeholders in the formulation of the authority's own strategies** – the City of Bradford introduced its community planning process in 1997. A draft plan was prepared as the basis of an extensive consultation exercise with a large number of local groups and organisations and was distributed to all households with a questionnaire. The results of the consultations and questionnaires were analysed and a final plan was produced which was subjected to further consultation at a series of area conferences designed to explore the implications of the plan

for each area within the City. The process was designed as a continuous one, so that the results of the area consultation were then fed into the preparation of the next year's draft plan with the whole process being repeated annually. The plan itself consisted of a statement of core values and five priority issues which are expressed in considerable detail explaining why the issue is considered to be a priority.

An example of a more selective approach has been the use of citizens' juries to assist in the exploration of strategic policy issues. (See Hall and Stewart, 1997, for an evaluation of the LGMB pilot projects.) The London Borough of Lewisham, for example, used this approach to help determine what the local authority could do to combat drug-related problems.

- **Involving local communities in developing neighbourhood plans for implementation by the authority** – Cambridge City Council is one of several authorities that has introduced ward or neighbourhood planning processes that involve local residents.
- **Involving external stakeholders in drawing up service, performance or business plans and in monitoring and reviewing service performance** – the extent and directness of involvement of external stakeholders varies considerably from one local authority to another. In some authorities involvement is limited to using the feedback received from service users and other stakeholders in the planning process. Other authorities, of which there are now many, have developed 'service panels' and user groups. Ipswich Borough Council has made extensive use of service panels in this way, and Clackmannanshire has gone even further by replacing traditional committees with a series of advisory groups.

The significance of these developments is that they represent attempts to open up both the planning and review of performance to a wider range of stakeholders. Performance is therefore something which is no longer to be determined and judged exclusively by the local authority – it becomes part of a wider democratic process. The emphasis placed on user and citizen inputs to the Best Value process will lead to a significant increase in the extent to which local authorities will need to include other stakeholders in the performance management process. Whether this will occur voluntarily or be imposed by the government remains to be seen.

There are, however, problems in developing a multiple stakeholder approach. There is already evidence that local authorities have had difficulties in reconciling aspirations of other stakeholders with their own political and professional views and requirements. Problems also occur in reconciling external views with budgetary constraints. Different stakeholders do not always speak with one voice, thereby creating further problems of reconciliation. Faced with these constraints, local authorities do not, and will not, find it easy to ensure that internal and external viewpoints are satisfactorily balanced in their decision making.

Making performance management systems work – some thematic issues

For the sake of clarity, each of the following thematic issues is presented as a pair of oppositional statements but it may be more appropriate for the reader to consider each as the ends of a continuum. The skill of performance management may therefore be expressed as knowing where best an organisation should be positioned on each continuum – and knowing how to design the systems and procedures that will take, and keep, the organisation there.

Top-down versus bottom-up

As performance management has been introduced in part as a response to the need to give a clearer direction and sense of purpose to a local authority, it can be implemented in a way that is excessively hierarchical and even autocratic in nature. Because the concept of performance management is based on the idea of cascading objectives down through the organisation, there is an inevitable tendency for this to happen. However, as local authorities have gained experience of performance management, they have learned that an exclusively top-down approach is less likely to result in a real sense of ownership of the objectives – and the plans and performance that result from them. They have therefore tried to develop corresponding bottom-up procedures to ensure that there is a counteracting force to this tendency. This makes the process more complicated but it is a much more realistic way of ensuring that performance, expectations and motivation are more closely related. The main mechanisms for achieving this dual approach vary but will typically include the following processes.

- Ensuring that the results of individual and team appraisal are fed back into the process for planning organisational performance.
- Ensuring that the strategic planning process includes a consideration of the competencies that will be needed in the organisation to implement the strategies.
- Quality circles and other similar ways of involving front-line staff in service improvements.

- Setting up planning processes at lower levels in the organisation, such as business unit, sectional, divisional and team plans, that are identifiable in their own right but are linked to the hierarchical strategic planning process.

The last of these four processes is the most important but also the most difficult to achieve. It requires the recognition that different planning processes need to influence one another – that planning performance should be seen as an *iterative* process, with planning being endemic at all levels with each level having an upward and downward influence on other levels.

Analysis and planning versus action and implementation

Some local authorities produce very good plans. At least they look good. But whether the apparent quality of the plan is reflected in the authority's competence in implementing it may be open to doubt. Planning needs to be balanced with implementation – the ability to ensure that the plans are acted upon. Analysis and action need to be balanced. In popular terms, the lack of balance may be seen either as 'paralysis by analysis' or as 'the unguided missile syndrome' (also known as 'load, fire, aim'). Perhaps the greatest danger for local authorities in this respect is where they organisationally separate the process of analysis and planning from that of implementation and action. While it is inevitable that large complex organisations need some degree of specialisation of the planning function, there is always the danger that 'specialism' becomes 'separation'. In effective biological systems the brain is always connected to the body – the same cannot be said of all research and planning units.

In recent years, the emphasis in government has been on action and results. A 'can do must do', 'what matters is what works' philosophy has permeated much of the public sector and initially at least this was a necessary antidote to the tendency for public services to develop long-term, grand master-plans, few of which became a reality. The pendulum has now swung in the opposite direction, with many organisations now more concerned with achieving apparently impressive short-term results than fully analysing issues in order to produce good solutions. To be seen to be doing something, perhaps anything, has become more important than ensuring that what you are doing is effective.

Planning as a process is too often conceived as the publication of a document with insufficient attention paid to the other parts of the process – defining the problem from the perspective of different stakeholders, collecting evidence and information, analysing the evidence and information and identifying and analysing possible solutions or options – all of which are necessary preconditions for producing a plan or solution that is likely to be effective.

Conformance and continuity versus challenge and change

There is a fundamental issue which is rarely explicitly addressed. Do organisations require conformance from their staff, especially in relation to following the requirements of some directive or plan, or do they want them to challenge that plan in the light of emerging events and knowledge? Put another way, is the purpose of planning performance to ensure that staff conform to the plan or is the plan intended as a baseline of anticipated actions and outcomes that needs to be continuously tested and challenged? The tension between these two objectives is unresolved in most organisations. Those which have more autocratic, top-down and bureaucratic planning processes will tend, implicitly or explicitly, to develop a culture which stresses conformance. The plan becomes an instrument of organisational control as much as a blueprint of the future intended direction of the organisation. Conversely an organisation that stresses participative, bottom-up, iterative styles of planning will, implicitly or explicitly, value challenges being made to existing plans. But the process of challenge has to be managed in relation to the process of planning. The aim is to produce an appropriate balance.

Continuity and change are also two ends of a continuum on which each organisation has to place itself. There is a strong pressure for continuity in all organisations and in public service ones in particular. The need to establish clear procedures in order to ensure public accountability and probity, and the need to ensure that public services are available as specified in standards and contracts, combine to force a local authority to give prominent attention to the processes it needs to have to ensure the continuity of service provision. The pressures for change are everywhere. They are not only external (for example, economic changes or changes in the needs of the community), they are also internal, with councillors and managers seeing themselves as agents of change. Determining an appropriate balance – between continuity and change – is another issue in managing performance.

Systems and procedures versus cultures and values

Descriptions of performance management, including the ones in this book, tend to dwell more on systems and procedures rather than the need to ensure that there are appropriate cultures and values.

Developing a 'performance oriented culture' has been the aim of some councillors and managers. But they have had a problem. Structures, systems and procedures are visible, physical manifestations of the organisation. They are consequently manipulable and can be changed. Cultures and values are not so obvious or evident. They appear to be resistant to change and they can sometimes change in a direction that is not intended. It is also evident that cultures cannot be changed as quickly as structures and systems and that different cultures emerge in different parts of complex organisations such as local authorities. Attempting to focus exclusively on cultures and values does not seem to work. Focusing exclusively on structures and systems certainly does not work. Where performance management has been most successful, it has been achieved through a balanced attention to both. In practice this has involved several factors:

- Involving staff in both the analysis of culture and in identifying ways it should and can be changed.
- Involving staff in the design of new systems and procedures.
- Ensuring that senior managers are closely involved with the implementation as well as the design of new systems and procedures.
- Being prepared to adapt systems in the light of cultural and value changes in the organisation.
- Ensuring that there is plenty of feedback throughout the organisation on how both cultures and systems are or are not changing or proving effective.

Conclusion

Most performance management systems focus primarily on what is happening inside the local authority – for the apparently obvious reason that the performance being managed and accounted for is that of the authority and its councillors and staff. In recent years, however, the idea that the performance of a democratically accountable unit of local government can be understood exclusively in terms of its performance in delivering the services for which it is directly and uniquely responsible has become increasingly challenged. It was initially challenged by academics (e.g. Stewart and Clarke, 1996), then by some local authorities (e.g. Kirklees, Bradford, Brighton and Hove, Lewisham) and more recently by the government (e.g. DETR, 1998a,b,c). Concepts of community leadership, community governance, community advocacy and democratic renewal have all been identified as part of the role of a local authority, in addition to its service delivery and regulatory roles. The acceptance of such roles dramatically changes the way in which the performance of an authority has to be viewed and, as a consequence, the systems and procedures for planning and reviewing it. Best Value and community planning are both proposals that may, in the future, radically change the way in which local authorities manage their performance.

7

The management of individual performance

Introduction

Some of the earlier writers on performance appraisal in this country such as V. and A. Stewart (1976 and 1977) defined the fundamental purpose of appraisal as being the alignment of the goals of the organisation with those of all the people who work within it. This simple definition remains as important today for two basic reasons.

- It explicitly recognises that individuals have goals and aspirations which they seek to realise while at work. If individuals have personal goals then it is reasonable to assume that they will engage in 'goal-seeking' behaviour and that this forms the basis of their performance.
- It recognises that organisations also have objectives – although, as was demonstrated in the previous chapter, they may be implicit rather than explicit. It is essential for organisational goals to be made explicit if they are to be aligned with those of its individual employees.

This chapter focuses primarily on performance appraisal because it is the process most associated with performance management. It explores the theories and assumptions that underpin the practice of performance appraisal and the problems and pitfalls that are commonly experienced in trying to make it work. It explores some of the approaches adopted in local government, including the issue of rewards and recognition before moving on to some recent and current developments.

Performance appraisal has become widely used in all types of organisations and it would be easy to conclude that it is perceived as a universal panacea – a management tool of incontestable value to all organisations. There is, however, considerable evidence that the benefits resulting from its use are far from universal and that, like all management techniques, it can either be well or poorly designed, implemented and sustained.

Performance appraisal in local government is currently undergoing a period of renewed interest. After the initial rush to introduce performance appraisal in the early 1980s there appeared to be something of a lull as authorities adjusted to the concept. In some cases it became an important part of a new management approach designed to focus attention on results and on improvement. In other authorities appraisal was gradually bureaucratised and assimilated into the traditional culture, while in yet others it withered away through neglect or as a result of direct resistance. The renewed interest in different forms of appraisal has been stimulated in some authorities by attempts to improve existing systems and in others by attempts to breathe new life into systems that had become moribund.

Throughout the chapter 'appraisal' and 'performance appraisal' are used as generic terms to describe systems that may be given labels such as 'staff development', 'staff appraisal', 'individual performance review' and 'joint review'.

Definitions and objectives

Moving beyond the basic definition of purpose given above, there are a variety of definitions in use. The Local Government Management Board defines appraisal in terms of four main activities: assessing past performance; reviewing plans for future performance; identifying training and development needs to improve contribution to current work; and clarifying career development prospects and planning to meet needs. (LGMB, 1993). The Audit Commission (1995b) suggests that appraisal has two main aims: to assist each employee to achieve a high standard of performance in the work which is necessary to enable their service and section to meet its own and the authority's aims and objectives; and to identify employees' training and development needs.

Several writers have noted the tendency for performance appraisal schemes to have a wide range of purposes and objectives. Rogers (1990) gives examples of 15 objectives found in local authority schemes:

- to identify employee strengths and weaknesses;
- to develop/train employees in their present jobs;
- to identify individuals for promotion;

- to plan career progression;
- to recognise good work;
- to provide a basis for salary progression/performance related pay;
- to establish and monitor performance objectives and targets;
- to clarify accountabilities and responsibilities;
- to alert managers to constraints which inhibit employee performance;
- to encourage/require managers to manage their staff in a systematic way;
- to develop communication between managers and their staff;
- to help develop a participative environment;
- to improve employee job satisfaction and motivation;
- to ensure equity in the treatment of employees
- to encourage self-evaluation. (Rogers, 1990)

Handy (1993) suggests that appraisal has four basic objectives:

- to provide a data base for the organisation's inventory of people, skills and potential;
- to provide a mechanism for performance to be properly assessed so that people may be appropriately rewarded;
- to provide individuals with feedback on performance and strengths and weaknesses;
- to help individuals plan personal and job objectives and ways of achieving them.

He goes on to point out, however, that even these four, although individually desirable, are not necessarily psychologically compatible and that the latter two are in any case difficult to do well. He recommends that the objectives should be fulfilled at different times using different means. Nonetheless, some local authorities incorporate as many as ten different objectives in their schemes, thereby causing confusion amongst their employees as to the primary objective and ignoring the possibility and consequences of incompatibility. While it is true that appraisal can contribute to a wide range of management processes, it is important to clarify which few purposes it has primarily been designed for. Schemes with multiple objectives tend to fail because appraisers adopt a selective, 'pick-and-mix approach' to the stated objectives, thereby imposing their own individual values, preferences and prejudices. Selecting a few primary objectives and then ensuring that any specified subsidiary objectives are compatible is in many ways the first and most important step in designing a scheme.

Some definitions of performance appraisal include a reference to rewards, and to performance related pay in particular, although such references are more common in American practice where salary decisions are seen as central to the credibility of appraisal. British writers more frequently emphasise the danger of creating too close a link with pay on the grounds that it overshadows and is detrimental to other useful purposes of appraisal (e.g. Anderson, 1993). One American survey found that approximately 90 per cent of organisations surveyed saw pay and rewards as the main purpose for appraisal (Eichel and Bender, 1984) despite the evidence from other studies that demonstrated linking pay review with performance appraisal was problematic (e.g. Meyer *et al.*, 1965). Although transatlantic differences in cultural assumptions and expectations require that such evidence be viewed with caution, the link to reward is nonetheless important in the context of British local government because of the encouragement given to performance related pay in the public sector by the government in the 1980s and its consequential introduction by a number of local authorities at the same time as they introduced performance appraisal. Indeed, in many authorities the two processes were integral parts of a new performance management regime. Most local authorities that have introduced and continue to use performance related pay tend to separate the award of payments from the appraisal process but it may be argued that the separation is perceived by many employees as artificial. The issues are explored later in the chapter.

Underlying theories

For the individual employee, performance management is essentially concerned with establishing a framework in which performance can be planned, organised, monitored, appraised and improved so that all employees can become as personally effective as possible. In doing this, managers have to have regard for the three main factors that determine personal effectiveness (see Figure 7.1): the *organisation*, as represented by its culture, systems, procedures, structure and, most importantly, its objectives; the *job*, in terms of its design, demands and complexity; and the *person*, in terms of his/her values, expectations, skills and experience. Combining these factors successfully is the main role of performance management. The main theoretical basis for this process is social psychology and in particular two theories of motivation, expectancy theory and goal-setting theory, together with the more general behavioural concepts of reinforcement theory.

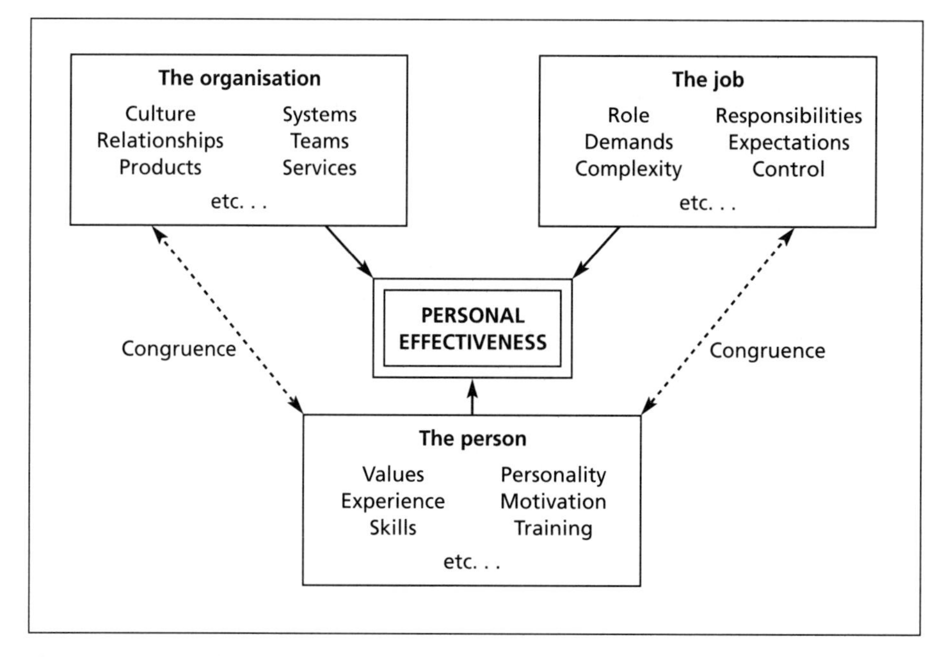

Figure 7.1 A model of personal effectiveness

Expectancy theory

Expectancy theory suggests that it is the anticipated satisfaction of valued goals that causes individuals to adjust their behaviour in a way that is most likely to lead to their achievement. Formulated initially by Vroom (1964), it has created enormous interest amongst both researchers and practitioners. It draws on a tradition that can be traced back to the Utilitarian philosophers, Mill and Bentham, who postulated a system of ethics in which individuals determined their actions by a conscious calculation of the expected consequences of those actions.

Expectancy theory explains motivation in terms of the outcome of three principal factors.

- *Expectancy* – an individual's own assessment of whether performing in a certain way will result in a measurable outcome for the individual.
- *Instrumentality* – the perceived probability that such an outcome will lead to the attainment of a specified reward.
- *Valence* – the individual's assessment of the likely satisfaction, or value, associated with the reward.

These factors are expressed diagrammatically in Figure 7.2 , from which it can be seen that two additional factors are necessary to explain the performance achieved – the organisational environment or influences that are external to the individual but which may determine an individual's ability to perform, and the individual's own skills, knowledge and experience. Put simply, expectancy theory suggests that individuals pose three fundamental questions when faced with some choice or requirement to act.

- What benefits can I get out of this if I do it? (The concept of expectancy.)
- What are the realistic chances of my actually obtaining those benefits? (The concept of instrumentality.)
- How much do I value what I am likely to get out of it? (The concept of valence.)

In practical terms, if an individual clearly sees that performing in a certain way will bring about a reward that is valued, then he/she is more likely to attempt to perform in that way than if the relationship between effort and measured performance, or performance and reward, is uncertain or unclear.

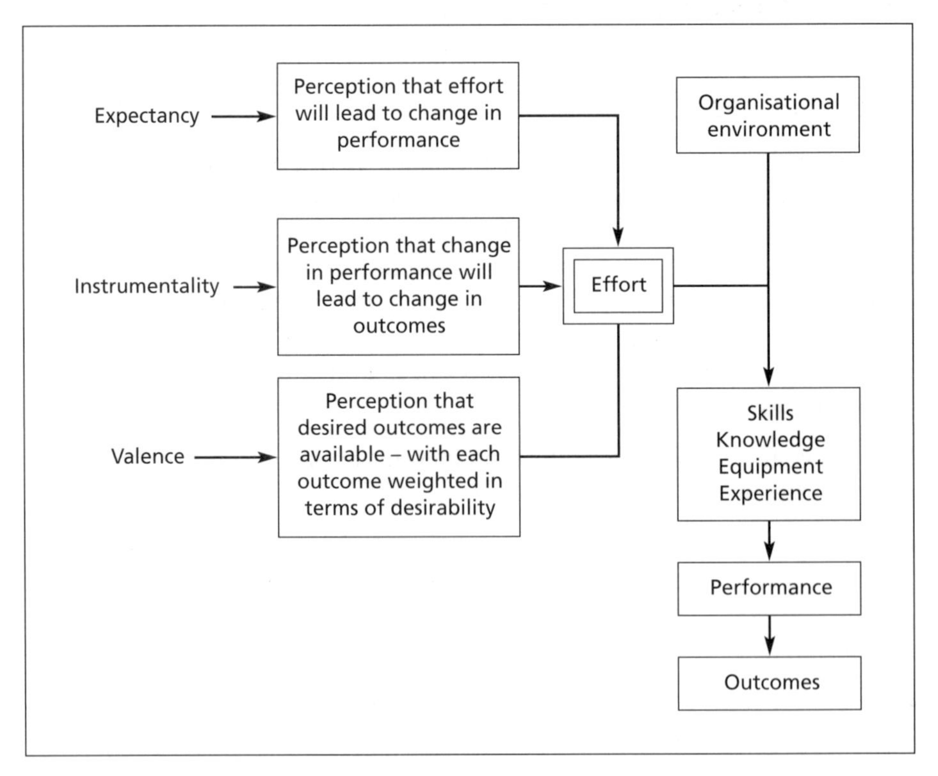

Figure 7.2 Motivation expectancy theory

Expectancy theory has been subjected to a great deal of empirical investigation that has generally produced fairly positive conclusions, although there have been a number of critics such as Campbell and Pritchard (1976). In so far as it is a reliable theory it poses some useful insights but also some problems for organisations in managing the performance of their employees. For example, if the expectations of employees vary significantly, the organisation is likely to have only the vaguest notion of what they are and will be unable to design working conditions and management systems that adequately reflect the variation. While appraisal provides an opportunity for organisations to learn more about their employees' expectations, it is doubtful whether many of them consciously and effectively utilise the opportunity. The theory also suggests that, if individuals have different perceptions of how best to achieve or satisfy their values, then the organisation has to learn how to cope with behaviours that may be variable and unpredictable. By providing time for discussion and dialogue, appraisal aims to create an opportunity for the organisation to learn why individuals behave and respond in the way they do – an opportunity which is more likely to be taken in those schemes that focus on the improvement of future performance than the achievement of past targets and objectives.

Goal-setting theory

Goal-setting theory was formulated by Locke in 1968 and was subsequently developed with other researchers (see, for example, Locke *et al.*, 1981; Locke and Henne, 1986; Mento *et al.*, 1987). Locke argued that the goals pursued by employees can play an important part in motivating them to achieve better performance. This is because in pursuing their goals people examine the consequences of their behaviour and, if they think that their goals will not be achieved with their current behaviour, they will either modify their behaviour or choose more realisable goals. If the aim of performance management and other HRM strategies is to achieve congruence between organisational and individual goals, then organisations that can make their employees perceive that it is worth their while pursuing the organisation's goals will be able to harness a strong source of motivation.

While the theory acknowledges that money is a primary incentive for most individuals it suggests that it is not the only incentive and does not necessarily motivate individuals to achieve better performance, other incentives can be provided through job enrichment and by personal and organisational development. Using evidence drawn from a range of experimental studies, Locke *et al.* (1981) formed the conclusion that goal setting appeared to be the most effective technique for achieving personal effectiveness and, as the theory was developed, it was found that a number of conditions needed to apply in order to make goal setting motivational. These have subsequently become the basis for good practice in performance appraisal.

- Goals should be specific and time related rather than vague and indefinite.
- Goals should be demanding, but also attainable and perceived as attainable.
- Feedback on performance is critical.
- Goals need to be accepted by employees as being personally valued and desirable.

Goal-setting theory has been subject to considerable empirical scrutiny and has stood up well to the test (see Locke and Henne, 1986), unlike other popular theories such as Maslow's Hierarchy of Needs (Maslow, 1954) and Hertzberg's Two Factor theory (Hertzberg, 1966), neither of which have been satisfactorily demonstrated empirically. In developing their theory of goal-setting Locke and Henne, while focusing primarily on the primacy of goals as instruments of motivation, constructed a broader model that includes all the factors that link motivation and performance (see Figure 7.3).

The model attempts to illustrate that:

- needs and their satisfaction are relevant to motivation but needs-based theories alone do not sufficiently explain human behaviour;
- personal values are also significant but, because they are difficult to measure and tend to change, they are not a sufficient way of explaining behaviour;
- emotions also have a part to play in the sense that 'satisfaction' is an emotion that results from individuals' appraisal of their achievement of their values and goals, but, because there is not an empirically demonstrable fixed relationship between individuals' emotions and their subsequent behaviour, theories that focus on emotions alone are unsatisfactory bases for explaining motivation.

Goal-setting theory therefore appears to be the best way of understanding the link between motivation and behaviour.

Goal-setting theory now provides a set of well tested principles which provide clear guidance to the designers of performance appraisal systems. Many local authority guides to performance appraisal draw directly, but perhaps unknowingly, on the theory.

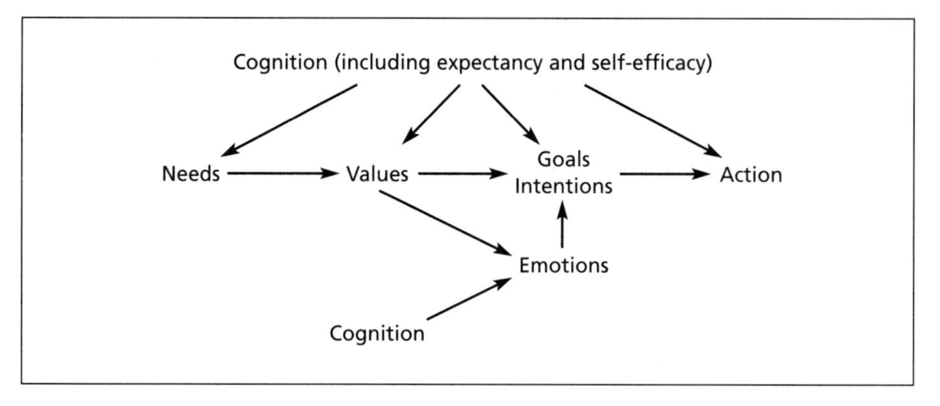

Figure 7.3 Performance and motivation
Source: Locke and Henne (1986)

Reinforcement theory

B.F. Skinner, a behavioural psychologist, concluded from his animal experiments that 'the behaviour that gets rewarded gets repeated' and in that simple statement lies much of the justification for performance related pay (PRP) and other performance reward systems. More importantly Skinner (1971), and other psychologists in the fields of educational and occupational psychology, have emphasised the value of *positive* reinforcement – that is the use of rewards, praise and other forms of reinforcement that are positively valued by the recipient. They found that positive reinforcement was more likely to create the changes (or continuities) of behaviour required than negative reinforcement (i.e. punishment or the withdrawal of rewards) which, although producing behavioural change, did so in an unpredictable and sometimes undesirable way. In other words, positive reinforcement works predictably, negative reinforcement works unpredictably. Peters and Waterman (1982) give the example of an employee punished for not treating a customer well. Not only may the employee not know how to 'treat a customer well' he may also react, not by seeking to improve the way in which he treats customers, but by seeking to avoid customers as much as possible – an alternative but logical way of avoiding the punishment which has resulted from his relationship with customers.

Positive reinforcement not only appears to work it can also have very positive and ethical characteristics. Like the concept of 'quality', nobody is against it and in the same way that Pirsig (1974) attributed Zen-like properties to quality, so positive reinforcement can strengthen other positive organisational characteristics.

Unfortunately, Skinner's ideas were strongly criticised because he later developed his theorising in a way that many people saw as ultimately manipulative. In concluding that people are simply a product of the stimuli they receive from their environment and that therefore, if the environment can be determined precisely enough, the future actions of all people can be precisely predicted, Skinner not only overstated the function of reinforcement but also raised many ethical questions. Fortunately, other adherents have been more measured in their claims for and use of the theory, but the ethical questions remain important when examining the way in which reinforcement theory is used not just in the workplace but also in other situations such as the classroom.

Within reinforcement theory, as with goal-setting theory, a number of conditions have been identified that help determine how effective reinforcement will be. These are:

- Reinforcement must be *specific* – a condition that is sometimes used to support results-based appraisal rather than behaviourally-based appraisal in situations where behaviour is more difficult to specify and/or observe.
- Reinforcement should be *immediate* – a condition that mitigates against the concept of once-a-year appraisals and reward systems that occur long after the behaviour or performance took place.
- Reinforcement should take account of the *achievability of desired behaviours* – a concept similar to that of setting realistic and achievable goals.
- Reinforcement can be *informal and almost intangible* – a smile or the lifting of an eyebrow can, in some circumstances, be as influential as formal rewards and punishments.
- *Unpredictable and intermittent* reinforcement works better than regular reinforcement which loses its impact because it becomes expected – this condition raises important questions about the way in which some PRP schemes have been operated in local government. The reward is often predictable and can be pre-determined by recipients with little reference to any changes in their behaviour.

Issues in appraisal

The ethics of performance appraisal

In 1990 Longenecker and Ludwig published an article in which they analysed why managers seek to exercise some 'creative discretion' over the way they rate and judge the performance of their staff. The research revealed that managers, who deliberately and knowingly inflate their ratings or judgements, and thereby manipulate the formal 'rules' of the appraisal process, do so on the basis of a number of ethically and morally based motives such as:

- a wish to avoid creating a negative permanent record that might have longer-term implications for the employee;
- a wish to avoid confrontation with 'difficult' employees;
- a desire to reward hard-working employees even when the results of their labours were poor;
- a desire to protect good performers whose performance had temporarily dipped because of factors beyond their control.

Other managers who admitted deliberately lowering their employees' ratings did so for the following kinds of reasons:

- to try to scare an employee into performing better;
- to encourage a problem employee to leave;
- to punish a difficult employee.

Longenecker and Ludwig suggested that managers who engage in deliberate inaccuracy may feel morally superior because they are doing so to achieve the broader purpose of appraisal – better motivation and performance – rather than following the narrower ethical requirements to be accurate. They propose a 'Janus-Headed' approach to appraisal in which both the organisation and the individual appraiser operate within a set of rights and obligations that seek to ensure that appraisal is conducted with accuracy, flexibility and sensitivity. Their solution is not wholly convincing, however, and highlights the fact that many managers do face moral dilemmas when appraising their staff – dilemmas which cannot always be resolved by improving the design of the appraisal process.

The Lake Wobegon Effect and the 'frotiling' syndrome

Critics of performance appraisal have argued that it will always remain an essentially subjective process despite the continuing search for methods and techniques that have the appearance of greater objectivity. One line of criticism is that while appraisal purports to be an objective and analytical process, at heart it is composed of a social process in which the relationship between the appraiser and the appraisee is of primary significance. As a consequence no matter how 'objectively' the scheme is designed, it becomes in practice a subjective social process. There is, for example, evidence that employees receive significantly higher ratings from appraisers of their own race (Kraiger and Ford, 1985) and that women working in traditionally male dominated organisations are likely to have their success attributed to luck, the easiness of the task or to their 'connections' rather than to their own abilities. Conversely their lack of success is more likely to be attributed to their personal characteristics. More generally, managers may feel uncomfortable in the appraiser role because it puts them in the position of playing 'God' (McGregor, 1960), and, as a consequence they may tend to cluster ratings around the average or give a higher rating than is warranted by the 'objective' level of performance.

A second line of criticism is based on evidence demonstrating that people in all kinds of situations tend to consider themselves 'above average'. This is true not just in the workplace but also social situations. Driving is a particularly good example of this tendency with a majority of drivers, particularly males, considering themselves above average, good or excellent. The personal need to feel good about oneself is a phenomenon described by Barkdoll (1989) as the 'Lake Wobegon Effect', taken from the author Garrison Keillor who ended each of his short stories with the following description of Lake Wobegon: 'Where all the women are strong, all the men are good looking, and all the children are above average.' If there is a social need to be 'better than average' then problems will be encountered in appraisals where this belief is not reinforced. This can result in perceptions and emotions not dissimilar to those experienced in another form of appraisal:

> *When I get a piece of work back and I think its good and I get a bad mark, I feel like frotiling the teacher. (Taken from Birmingham Education Department's guidelines on assessing student performance. Undated)*

Given free will and choice most appraisers will seek to avoid circumstances that may result in them being 'frotiled', and appraisees will always seek to put forward their achievements in the best possible light in order to avoid the negative emotional feelings that result from a poor appraisal.

Conversely there is the well-known saying that 'we are our own worst critic', implying that individuals criticise themselves more severely than others. Advocates of the concept of self-appraisal have used the evidence that supports this to promote their ideas and some appraisal schemes are based on the principle that the starting point of the process should be the appraisee's own evaluation of their performance. In fact there is a good deal of mixed evidence as to whether individuals are severe or lenient on themselves and the only general conclusion that can probably be drawn is that the circumstances in which appraisal takes place have an important influence on the degree of leniency or severity which occurs in self-appraisal.

Where individuals are asked to assess their performance in relation to different aspects of their job, rather than to compare themselves against other employees, evidence suggests that they are more discriminating in their judgements than their managers and that their assessments are also realistic and 'objective'. Expectancy theory would suggest that individuals calculate the personal consequences of being more or less self-critical and respond accordingly. There may however be a difference between the extent to which individuals are able to be self-critical to themselves and the degree to which they are prepared to do so publicly. 'Blame' cultures do not promote public self-appraisal. The resulting problem for the appraiser is that the appraisee's behaviour may be a response to a private self-criticism that is different to the publicly stated self-appraisal – thereby making it difficult for the appraiser to suggest appropriate reinforcing or remedial action.

Feedback, learning and systems thinking

Theory also suggests that the ability of the individual to be 'accurately' self-critical depends on the feedback they have on their own performance. Such feedback comes in many forms. As described in Chapter 4, the stories told and pictures painted of performance can consist of statistics or of narrative and may be formal or informal. In some occupations feedback is immediate and part of the job, in other cases it has to be constructed, recorded and fed back at a later date. Appraisal provides an opportunity to bring together different forms of feedback and for it to be effective it is important that a balance is achieved between the different forms.

Feedback is a systems concept and 'performing' is a dynamic rather than a static process. It therefore requires feedback that is dynamic in the sense of being responsive to all the changes occurring in the system, some of which may relate to organisational requirements and circumstances, others to changing customer expectations and yet others to changes within the person being appraised. Inappropriate feedback that does not reflect the current dynamics of the system can be confusing or result in inappropriate responses. But lack of feedback can be even worse because without feedback systems go out of control. Feedback is the process by which individuals and organisations learn about what is happening – and as a consequence change their behaviour appropriately. Appraisal can therefore be seen as an organisational fall-back device to ensure that all employees receive at least some feedback on a regular basis. On its own it is likely to be insufficient but if all other processes have failed, it prevents the total absence of personal feedback.

The importance of feedback and the variety of ways it can be given and received has been illustrated in the context of equal opportunities. Here it has been demonstrated that members of minority social, ethnic and gender groups can have less idea of how their performance is perceived and judged than members of the majority group because valuable feedback is given in informal social situations to which the minority groups are not party. In traditional male-dominated organisations the 'nod that's as good as a wink' is as likely to be given in the pub, on the golf course or in the men's toilet as it is in the appraisal interview.

There is, however, a substantial amount of evidence indicating how feedback can be used effectively in appraisal and the following points are all crucially important.

- The amount of critical (i.e. negative) feedback should be limited. Some studies have shown that in unsuccessful appraisals the appraisers spend a higher proportion of the time either criticising or disagreeing with the appraisees than in successful appraisals.
- A balanced view of performance, with attention being given to strengths as well as weaknesses, is also a characteristic of appraisals having useful outcomes.
- Feedback should be clear, relevant and should focus on the performance of the appraisee rather than their personal characteristics.
- All other sources of feedback should be made available and used in the appraisal – even if they are already known – because they contribute to the creation of a full picture of performance.
- Encouraging and using the appraisee's own feedback on performance has also been shown to be a crucial characteristic of successful appraisal.
- Giving feedback must not be limited to the occasional appraisal interview. There is consistent evidence showing that those managers who continuously give good feedback and frequently communicate have the most productive appraisals.

Judging and developing

Despite the best endeavours of the designers of appraisal systems it has to be accepted that, with the exception of very simple individual tasks that can be very tightly defined, appraisal will always contain some element of subjectivity on the part of both appraiser and appraisee. That however is not an argument for dispensing with it. If one of the problems of making complex organisations work effectively is the range of conflicting expectations and messages about performance that are held by different people in the organisation, then a form of appraisal that focuses more on a mutual dialogue aimed at establishing common expectations (and, consequentially, focuses less on the appraisal or rating of one person by another), can still be a very useful addition to the mechanisms used for managing performance. This approach to appraisal is now reflected in some local authorities, as the following extract from an internal report indicates:

> *I would suggest that Performance Appraisal is rather a limiting and possibly contentious phrase and that the term 'Joint Review' could be used to describe the process more adequately whereby a manager and an employee could come together to discuss the employee's past and present work performance and future expectations....To manage effectively, those who are responsible for employees should consult and encourage joint participation in deciding goals. Through this process individual personal development can be harmonised with the overall objectives of the City Council.*

From recruitment to organisational culture to appraisal

Using an appraisal process to align organisational and individual objectives could be viewed by some readers as an attempt to close the stable door after the horse has bolted. If organisations employ individuals whose values and goals are fundamentally in conflict with those of the organisation then the possibility of realignment may be limited or even non-existent.

Appraisal is not the only method used to create alignment. Selection procedures, for example, are used not just to identify individuals who have the required skills and experience but also to identify individuals who have similar goals, values and expectations to those of the organisation. To achieve this end, psychologists have devised an array of tests which claim to assess personal characteristics such as personality, aptitude and motivation and these are used, with other evaluative and judgmental methods, to assess the suitability of individuals not just in terms of their capacity to do specified jobs but their suitability as members of the organisation. Some local authorities use assessment centres employing a battery of tests that claim to be highly reliable in achieving a better fit between the recruit, the job and the organisation, although the extent to which they do so in practice is obviously open to some question. No matter how good the methods of recruitment are, the compatibility between employee, job and organisation is unlikely to remain stable for long for the simple reason that organisations, jobs and individuals can change quite radically in even a relatively short space of time. The organisation therefore needs processes which constantly seek to maintain the level of compatibility – thereby providing a justification for performance appraisal.

Organisations also seek to manage their culture so as to ensure that it is appropriate to the environment, to their objectives and aspirations and to the self-image of their owners and senior managers. It may be argued that, to be effective, performance appraisal needs to reflect the prevailing culture and that one of the primary reasons for its ineffectiveness is where it is perceived to be in conflict with, or irrelevant to, that culture. But, at the same time, it is evident that some local authorities have introduced appraisal as part of a package of change intended to radically transform the culture of the organisation. This presents something of a conundrum: should appraisal reflect the prevailing culture or can it be part of the process of changing that culture? The answer is that it can and has been used in both ways. Appraisal may be linked to new or improved processes for strategic, service and business planning, to more extensive forms of service review, and to improved communication and reporting systems, all of which are designed to produce a culture which is more focused on performance and open to reflection and learning.

Radical cultural change may have become more necessary in the public sector but it is not easy to manage, as Pettigrew *et al.* (1993) have demonstrated with regard to the NHS. Two of the difficulties experienced in trying to transform the cultures of organisations is that, in addition to being resistant to change, cultures change rather more slowly than many managers would like. Real change in culture occurs over a long period of time during which constant reinforcement and reiteration of the 'change message' has to take place. The systems that have been introduced as part of the change need to be carefully managed and monitored if they are to become bedded down into the organisation. However, in some organisations the attention span of managers is too short for this to be done properly. Having introduced the system, they move on to other aspects of change. An appraisal system, if it is to successfully support cultural change, must be continuously supported and sustained by managers and, when appropriate, adjusted in response to other organisational changes.

Some final thoughts on theory and practice

The basic problem faced by the designers and participants in appraisal and reward systems is knowing what assumptions and expectations are held by all participants. Each of the theories outlined, along with other theories such as social comparison theory (Festinger, 1951), contribute something to our understanding of human motivation but none of them, even goal-setting theory which has been given pride of place in this context, fully explain either motivation or the behaviour which results from it. All the theories rest on *assumptions* about human nature in general and about the nature of the environment in which we live and work. Because they also seek to predict the behavioural consequences of motivation they inevitably raise moral and ethical questions about free will, self-control, self-determination and manipulation.

Management systems such as performance appraisal and reward inevitably draw on these theories and at the same time provide the empirical evidence from which new theories are developed – the two often go hand-in-hand. Those who design and participate in such systems need to understand that they are inevitably crude mechanisms, of which some organisations and managers nonetheless have over-ambitious expectations. Appraisal is just one additional process to add to the formal and informal motivational toolkits used to manage individual performance.

Performance appraisal in local government

The first edition of this book (Rogers, 1990) identified three categories of appraisal being used in local government.

- Developmental schemes, focusing on the developmental and training needs of staff.
- Performance improvement schemes, focusing on continuous improvement in meeting performance objectives and targets.
- Reward based appraisal schemes, used as the basis for the allocation of rewards and comprising three categories – schemes for promotion and regrading, bonus incentive schemes and performance related pay schemes.

Randall *et al.* (1984), looking at appraisal in a wider range of organisations, created a not dissimilar threefold categorisation of potential reviews, performance reviews and reward reviews and advocated the use of all three in a single organisation. I also indicated that during the 1980s there had been a movement away from schemes in my first category towards the second and this is partly reflected in the two major surveys of appraisal in UK organisations carried out during that period. Figure 7.4 shows that setting performance objectives had increased markedly as one of the main purposes of appraisal, at the expense of career planning and the assessment of potential – shifts that can be accounted for by the changed economic environment and the increasing challenge to assumptions about the continuity and stability of patterns of employment.

Since 1990 there appears to have been a trend in local government towards the integration of the first two categories. In moving in this direction, local authorities are trying to combine in a single scheme a highly objective, results and target based form of appraisal with an equally sharp focus on the development of staff competencies and skills. While this looks to be a rational and logical development, the success of such schemes in achieving their broader range of objectives will be dependent on a number of critical factors.

	1977 %	1985 %
To assess training needs	96	97
To improve current performance	92	97
To review past performance	91	98
To assess future potential	87	71
To assist career planning decisions	81	75
To set performance objectives	57	81
To assess salary increases	39	40

Figure 7.4 Main purpose of performance appraisal
Source: Gill (1977) & Long (1986)

First, there is the problem of ensuring that these multiple objectives can be designed into a scheme so that they are mutually compatible; second, there is the practical problem of appraisers and appraisees having the capacity to cope with the complexity created by multiple objectives; and third, there is the problem that these more complex schemes are dependent on the existence of a learning culture which values and supports the development of competencies and skills within the organisation rather than their acquisition by means of external recruitment. Such a culture needs to be sustained by making resources available for training and development. While there is evidence of an increased strategic approach to learning and employee development, of which the interest in attaining Investors in People status is one example, it is also the case that, in comparison to other sectors, local government still spends a low proportion of its resources on training and development.

The model on which many current appraisal schemes are based is illustrated in Figure 7.5. It consists of six main elements.

- **Defining the job: accountabilities and competencies** – some of the objectives and results based schemes introduced in the 1980s, especially those for managers, commenced with a redefinition of each job in terms of its primary accountabilities. This was achieved through job evaluation procedures carried out by the local authority or by the management consultants employed to design the appraisal scheme. More recently, there appears to have been less concern for ensuring that jobs are well designed and evaluated, with local authorities responding to resource constraints by simply attaching new responsibilities to existing jobs without any great concern for whether the resulting job is logical and realistic. But there has been a noticeable trend towards defining jobs, particularly those of a

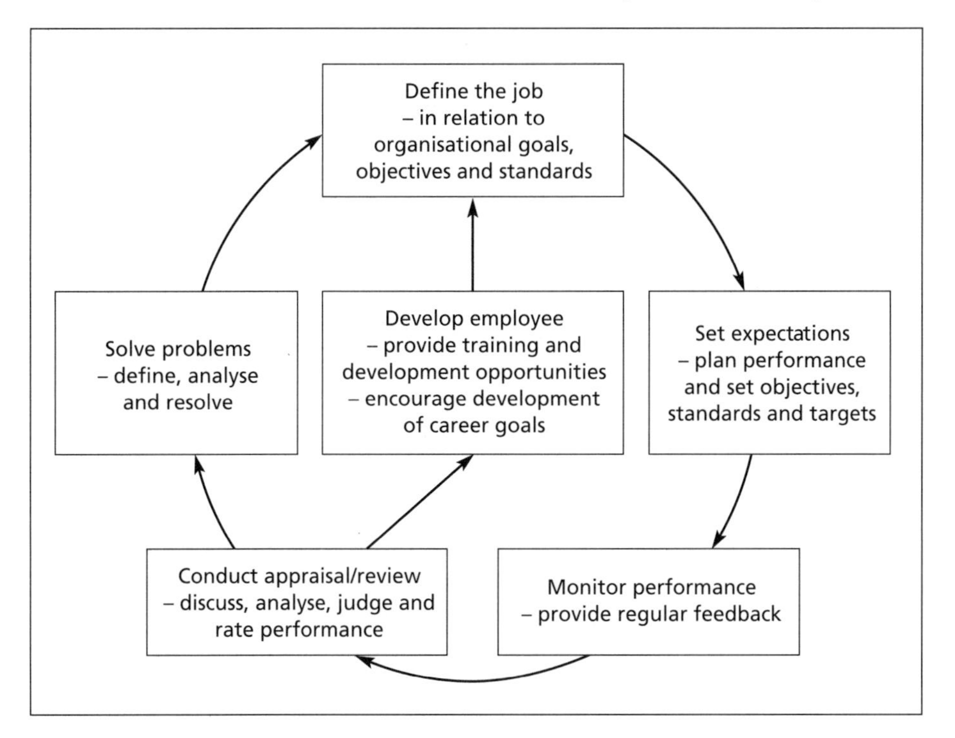

Figure 7.5 The performance appraisal/development cycle

technical or administrative nature, in terms of the competencies required to fulfil them and it is likely that the move towards single status employment and the associated introduction of the LGMB job evaluation scheme will lead to a renewed interest in this aspect of the appraisal process.

- **Setting expectations: objectives, standards and targets** – this aspect of performance appraisal remains the core activity in many schemes but in practice can be poorly conducted, with little regard for ensuring that organisational and individual objectives are aligned as closely as possible. Targets also tend to be set more in terms of volume, speed and efficiency of performance than effectiveness and quality. These problems are discussed below.

- **Monitoring performance and providing feedback** – while many schemes formally refer to the need to ensure that performance is regularly monitored and fed back to the appraisee, the extent to which this is done in practice varies considerably. This is usually not a failure of the scheme itself but of those managers who use the existence of annual appraisals as an excuse for not providing regular feedback.

- **Conducting appraisals** – most schemes provide for an annual appraisal with some also incorporating a mid-year or quarterly review. Many schemes also ensure that all employees involved in them are given some form of training in how appraisals should be conducted and evidence suggests that such training is essential. However, some training focuses only on the mechanics of the appraisal scheme and ignores several problem areas such as how to set good objectives, how to ensure that appraisals are balanced and how to deal with performance problems. There appears to be an implicit assumption in some local authorities that if appraisals are carried out correctly there will be no ensuing performance problems.
- **Develop employee** – some local authorities have become much more focused in their strategic approach to training and development by combining the information emerging from the appraisal process with an analysis of the competencies needed by the organisation to fulfil its specification of mission and strategic priorities. There has also been more attention given to the use of internal developmental initiatives – as distinct from external training programmes. But in other authorities the decentralisation of training budgets has led to an inability to meet identified needs and a lack of corporate capacity to lead and promote major training and development initiatives.
- **Solving problems** – this, as suggested above, may often be the weakest part of formal schemes. It is often assumed that individual managers have the skills to resolve those performance problems that have not been resolved within the appraisal process. But it is these residual problems which are the most intractable and require the greatest skill and support for them to be resolved. Managers need more support than is often available in order to help them explore potential solutions rather than prematurely resorting to disciplinary action.

Formalisation of appraisal schemes

The extent to which schemes are formalised and documented varies and there is always a difficult decision to make in this respect. Highly defined schemes can easily become bureaucratised with the consequence that the primary purpose becomes the completion of the paperwork arising from it. Figure 7.6 provides an example of a highly defined process which, although containing many good ideas such as learning contracts, is highly prescriptive and bureaucratic. By contrast, Cambridgeshire County Council, which was one of the first authorities to introduce a results based appraisal scheme in the early 1980s, provides a manual that focuses on giving advice on how to approach each step in the process rather than on its more mechanical aspects.

The manual has been regularly updated to reflect the improvements that have been made over the years and its current version contains a number of developments such as personal development plans, competencies, benchmarking and 360 degree review (Cambridgeshire, 1996).

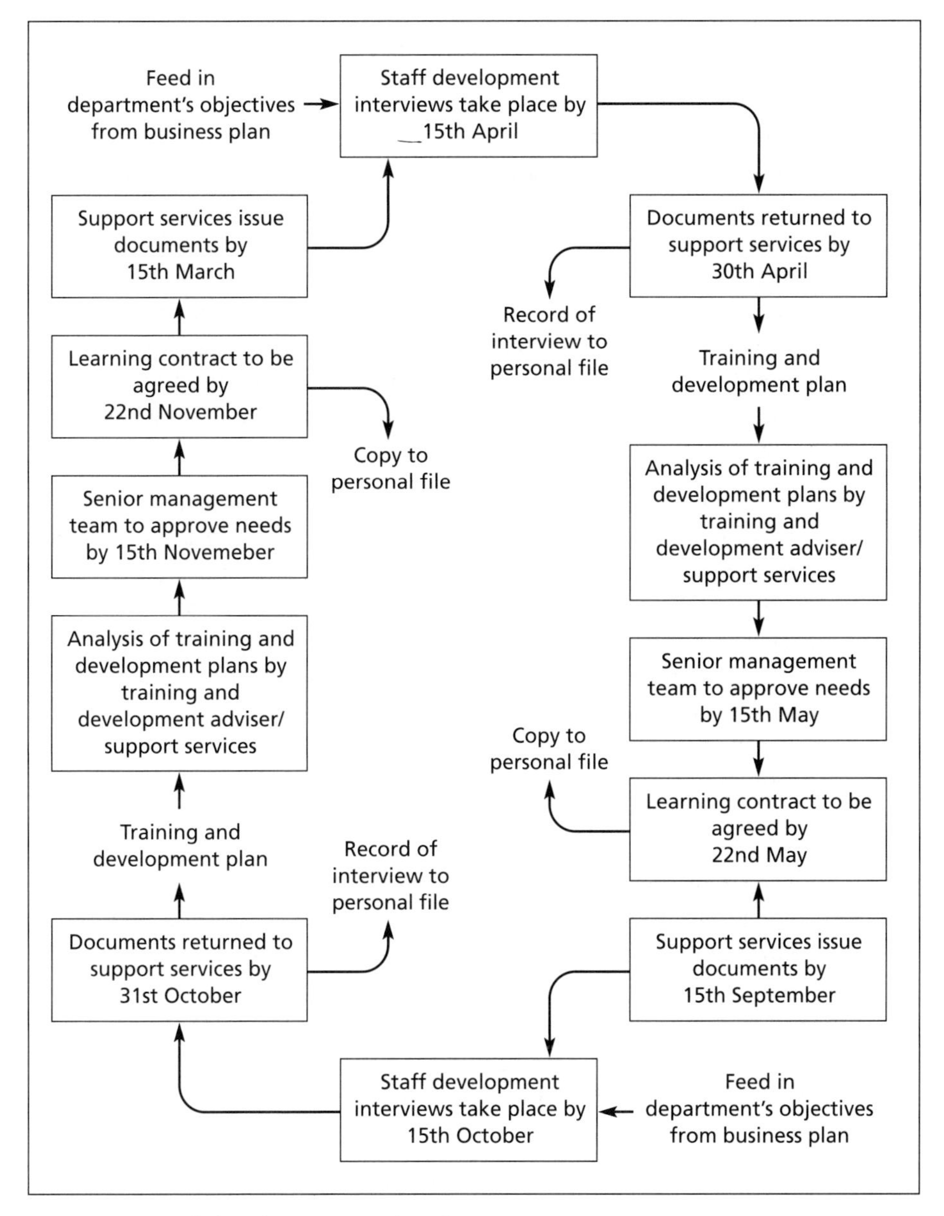

Figure 7.6 Staff development and review

Source: Humberside County Council: Staff Development and Review Scheme, March 1994

Appraisal problems and pitfalls

The purpose of this section is to highlight some of the problems that emerge when using appraisal in local government.

Setting objectives and targets – what and who's performance?

In some appraisal systems managers are used as surrogates for the organisation they manage – the objectives and targets set for them are the same as for the organisation. In such cases targets will be set in terms of, for example, ensuring that budgets are met or that departmental projects are completed on time and are justified on the grounds that the manager is ultimately responsible for them – even if he or she does little of the work involved in delivering the result. But to appraise managerial effectiveness it is necessary to examine what a manager personally contributes to the achievement of the organisational target – and that means setting objectives and targets that relate to what managers do as managers, how they behave and what competencies they display.

The way in which performance contracts for chief and other senior officers have been developed in Birmingham City Council is a good example of this problem. The contracts are the basis of a form of annual appraisal in which the Chief Executive discusses and agrees a set of performance objectives and targets for each chief officer that are then cascaded down amongst senior managers in each department. In the early years of the process the chief officers' objectives and targets related to the performance of their departments rather than to them as individuals. Objectives generally were of two kinds – service and policy targets on the one hand, and targets relating to the general management of the department and the authority on the other. After several years of operating in this way the chief officers began to point out that this approach gave, at best, an indirect indication of their own personal contribution to the City Council and the process was adapted, by using a 'balanced scorecard approach', to include objectives and targets that related more to their personal contribution. (See Figure 7.8 and the section on p. 144 for more details of the balanced scorecard.) In other local authorities this problem has been addressed through the use of competencies, using either those contained in national systems such as the Management Charter Initiative or by developing their own framework of competencies.

In formulating objectives and targets for individuals it is important to address five key questions.

- What does the organisation want the individual to achieve?
- What does the organisation want the individual to do?
- How does the organisation want the individual to behave?
- What competencies does the individual need to possess and demonstrate?
- What personal objectives does the individual want to achieve?

Looked at in this way the process of objective setting becomes more sensitive and realistic but at the same time more complex – the appraisers cannot just take a set of objectives or targets from a service or business plan and mechanistically allocate them amongst their staff. The process requires planning, thoughtfulness, it is time-consuming and the objectives and targets set will not all be easy to monitor and review. In other words, the appraiser and the appraisee have to think 'in the round' about their contribution to the organisation.

In appraising managers it is helpful to distinguish between four types of objectives.

- *Service or business objectives* – these relate to organisational performance and can usually be drawn from corporate, service and business unit plans.
- *Management objectives* – these relate to the way in which the organisation and its resources are to be managed. They may be contained in formal plans but may also need to be formulated specifically for each manager.
- *Management competencies* – these relate to the specified skills and behaviours that the organisation expects the manager to demonstrate in carrying out his job.
- *Personal objectives* – these are the personal development and career development goals of the individual manager.

Achieving balance in appraisals

Appraisals can, as already stated, be unbalanced in a number of ways. They are more likely to produce effective outcomes where appraisers seek to ensure a sense of balance in each of the following dimensions.

- Between the main elements of the appraisal process – i.e. planning, objective and target setting; monitoring performance; and evaluating or appraising performance.
- A time-related balance – ensuring that the appraisee's performance over the whole period of time under review is taken into account.
- A balance between the contribution of the appraisee and appraiser in the interview.

- A balance between reflection, judgement, problem-solving and coaching. This is a requirement that is easy to state but difficult to achieve, requiring immense skill on the part of the appraiser.
- A balance between discussing the most and least successful aspects of the appraisee's performance.

Judgement problems

Not all appraisers are skilled in observing behaviour, in recalling it, in interpreting its causes and effects or in determining its effectiveness. It is therefore not surprising that they feel uncomfortable and unsure about undertaking this task – feelings that may be exacerbated if the criteria to be used in judging performance are unclear or contestable. At worst (or best?) such feelings may be alleviated by the circulation of comic appraisal guides such as that in Figure 7.7. Skill, practice and support are needed to help appraisers distinguish between what people achieve, what they do and what personal characteristics they possess. One important aid to judgement is the development of competency frameworks which provide a more precise and rounded set of criteria within which discussions and judgements of performance can take place.

Common errors that arise in rating performance

There is considerable research based literature on the errors that commonly arise when appraisers rate the performance of their appraisees. Although the frequency with which some of these errors are likely to arise can be reduced through the improved design and monitoring of appraisal schemes, because it is impossible to make the process entirely objective, some errors will continue to arise. James (1988) summarises the main kinds of error as follows.

- *Halo effect* – where rating on one quality or objective influences ratings for others.
- *Leniency/severity effect* – the general tendency to assign extreme ratings.
- *Error of central tendency* – the tendency to rate all individuals 'safely' in the middle of a scale.
- *Contrast effect* – the tendency to rate individuals in relation to other employees rather than in relation to the requirements of the job.
- *Similarity effect* – the tendency for appraisers to rate those they see as similar to themselves more highly than others.
- *First impression error* – the tendency for initial evaluations to overshadow subsequent performance.

Performance	*Outstanding*	*Highly capable*	*Average*	*Sub-standard*	*Totally incapable*
Dexterity	Vaults over canyons with the greatest of ease	Leaps rivers after a running start	Can jump ditches with a following wind	Falls into ditches	Ditches colleagues for own ends
Mental capabilities	Thinks quicker than lightning	Thinks	Avoids thinking	Needs to avoid thinking	Requires a brain transplant
Efficiency	Catches rockets in flight with bare hands	Moves as fast as a rocket	Would you believe a slow rocket?	Needs frequent rockets	Accidental suicide
Resourcefulness	Walks on water	Only occasionally gets wet feet	Manages to stay in the swim	Cannot keep his head above water	Passes water in emergencies
Negotiation ability	Argues with the angels	Argues with Sir Robin	Argues with himself	Loses arguments with himself	Cannot understand himself
Personal attributes	As strong as a bull	Amateur matador	Talks bull	Thinks like a bull	Smells like a bull
Managerial ability	God-like	Believes in God	Plays God	Believes he IS God	God!
Recommended action	Hide this assessment from the Chief Executive	Watch out for	Sweat	Recommend for inter-departmental transfer	Ready for recruitment by a competitor

Figure 7.7 A guide to the appraisal of subordindates

Source: Unknown (given to the author by a senior manager)

- *Recency error* – the tendency, often resulting from insufficient preparation and monitoring, for greater weight to be given to the most recent performance.
- *Over-dependence on a single source* – the tendency to rely on a limited number of objectives, targets and behaviours that do not reflect the whole of an individual's performance.
- *Cognitive errors* – which may relate either to the memory limitations of the appraiser or to a failure or inability to monitor adequate information about the individual's performance.

- *Causal attributions* – raters may vary in the way they comprehend and explain the causes of good or bad performance, using either *external* causalities (i.e. the contextual or situational factors which may have influenced or determined an individual's performance) or *internal* causalities (i.e. the characteristics, skills and competencies of the individual).
- *Stereotyping* – the use of oversimplified and sometimes inaccurate assumptions about particular groups in society which then influence the rating of individuals from those groups.

Raising the organisational iceberg – discussibles and non-discussibles

One of the problems with appraisal is that, while it is based on the premise that it is important for managers and their staff to put time aside for direct, face-to-face dialogue, the culture and managerial style of some organisations do not really value or support such an approach. Some bureaucratic organisations rely more on paper and electronically based forms of communication. Some managers work hard at avoiding personal contact with their staff, preferring to communicate by memo, telephone and e-mail. The appraisal interview is therefore an unwelcome intrusion on their management style, to which they react adversely. Gender problems can ensue where managers perceive appraisal as an opportunity for a 'no-holds-barred, man-to-man talk'. Issues of ethnicity can arise for employees from ethnic groups where praise and criticism are given in coded and oblique forms that can only be fully appreciated by members of that group. The way something is said may be as important as what is said.

The culture of some organisations prohibits discussion of some issues that are of importance to organisational performance. At worst, like an iceberg, only a small proportion is above water and out in the open. Management teams can be very good at constructing conversational icebergs in which insignificant issues become the basis of discussion while issues of greater importance to the effective performance of the local authority go undiscussed. Organisations create their own rules and expectations for discourse. In some management teams discussion of principles is permitted but not an analysis of how each member of the team is putting the principles into practice. In other teams the focus is reversed – a focus on results with no framework of values or principles. Some teams allow facts but not emotions The more that is non-discussible the more difficult it is to effectively manage performance.

Appraisal can help in raising the iceberg by redefining what should and should not be discussed. By providing an opportunity to discuss expectations, results, behaviours, competencies, aspirations and values in a structured way it helps organisations to focus on the more important determinants of performance.

Reward and recognition

The apparently inexorable trend towards the introduction of performance related pay (PRP) in local government appears to have come to an end and has even been put into reverse with some local authorities disbanding their schemes and others amending them. There continues to be a fierce debate about its effects on motivation and performance improvement. Part of this debate is, in reality, something of a sham for the main determinants of whether local authorities use PRP are more to do with economics than psychology. Nonetheless the motivational debate continues, based more on opinion than clear empirical evidence. Ethical considerations have also had a part to play in the debate, with the tendency of top managers and directors in the private sector, and especially the privatised utilities, to award themselves large performance bonuses that may be only indirectly related to their contribution to their company's current performance. The 'Cedric Brown' syndrome may in fact have had more impact on the move away from PRP in local government than either economic or psychological arguments.

The mixture of psychological and economic influences on PRP are well illustrated by the Audit Commission's 1995 study. Having at an earlier stage supported PRP the Commission was, by 1995, no longer convinced of all aspects of its merits. While asserting that performance management generally had a positive impact on staff motivation they were unconvinced as to the positive effect of PRP.

> *There is no evidence to suggest that pay itself improves motivation – moreover poor implementation of PRP can cause resentment and demotivate staff. (Audit Commission, 1995). The Commission goes on to say that:*
>
> *even if pay does improve performance ... the impact in local government may be small because public sector employees appear to be less driven by pay considerations than those employed in the private sector (supported by the IPM's recent report,* ***Performance Management in the UK****)... and because... PRP settlements in local authorities are generally small ... because local government staff are rarely able to generate increased income to fund the payment. (Audit Commission, 1995).*

The Commission acknowledges that if local authorities wish to develop more flexible pay systems then they will 'inevitably' need to give consideration to PRP.

This perhaps reflects the author's earlier view that the system of national pay grades created little relationship between pay and either achievement or effort and that some local authorities:

> *... perhaps encouraged by the government's attitude towards national pay bargaining, and influenced by the prevailing climate of escalating remuneration levels for senior managers in the private sector (had), adopted the ... solution of introducing Performance Related Pay based, in a number of cases, on broadly determined pay bands and term contracts. (Rogers, 1990)*

The Local Authorities' Conditions of Service Advisory Board (LACSAB, 1990) had undertaken research into the newly created PRP schemes and found that, while not perfect, they did motivate staff and also led to an improved analysis and integration of objectives and activities at different organisational levels. Some years on it is necessary to question whether these benefits resulted from the introduction of PRP in particular or from other aspects of performance management. The Audit Commission's view that local authorities must 'inevitably' give consideration to PRP is therefore open to doubt.

In reality the Commission's change of view was more clearly grounded on a set of economic rather than motivational arguments. The Commission demonstrated that the conditions of the local government labour market had substantially changed by 1995. Some local authorities had introduced PRP in the 1980s as a response to recruitment and retention difficulties with the consequence that there was little direct relationship between pay and performance in the way the schemes had been designed. The primary purpose of such schemes was to provide a more attractive remuneration package than could be provided within the national pay grades. Relating pay directly to performance was of only secondary interest. By the mid 1990s the Commission had evidence that not only was the total paybill of local authorities increasing but it was increasing most amongst senior staff – the staff who had been the main recipients of PRP schemes.

Despite several research projects and even after over ten years of use in local government, not enough is known about the motivational aspects of PRP to draw any firm and generalisable conclusions. The arguments are characterised as much by assertion as by any real attempt to generate evidence – a problem exacerbated by the fact that it is difficult to obtain reliable evidence. The LACSAB study, although very thorough in relation to the design and application of PRP schemes, was rather less thorough in its attempts to evaluate the results of such schemes. Interviews with senior managers who were the primary recipients of performance payments not surprisingly produced a strong vote in favour of their real, assumed or imagined benefits. Like any individual management technique or process it is very difficult to distinguish the benefits resulting from PRP from all the other influences on staff motivation and performance. In local government PRP has tended to be introduced as part of a package of organisational change and it is methodologically very difficult to separate the impact of PRP from the impact of other aspects of the package. It would, however, be illuminating to find out if the advocates of schemes that were designed as part of recruitment and retention packages have claimed the same performance benefits as those who designed schemes that did try to explicitly link pay to performance.

There has also been considerable discussion about the relationship between PRP and appraisal and the separation of the two in operation and time was supported by an IPM study (Gill, 1977). Long's (1986) later study for the IPM found that there had only been a marginal increase in the proportion of organisations using appraisal to directly determine salary increases. Anderson (1993) noted a growing tendency to relate performance appraisal to pay and predicted that there would be a rise in the proportion of organisations doing so. Generally however the predominant view in the UK appears to be in support of separation, as reflected by the Audit Commission:

> *it is now considered good practice to separate personal appraisal interviews for performance and development assessment from those for performance pay settlements. This is because consideration of the pay element can undermine the need for open and honest discussion that is a prerequisite for successful personal appraisal. (Audit Commission, 1995b)*

The Advisory, Conciliation and Arbitration Service supported this view on similar grounds (ACAS, 1990). But the question remains as to whether, even if the mechanics of the two processes are separated, they are viewed as being independent of each other by employees – particularly where it is the same manager who conducts the appraisal and makes the judgement about pay.

The argument and the evidence lead to perplexity. Is PRP a good thing or not? The only realistic answer is that other things being equal, it should create more benefits than costs if it is possible to design and to regularly update and sustain a scheme that meets the following conditions.

- The reward is clearly linked, and proportionate to, the effort made and the results achieved by recipients.
- Clear, fair, consistent and understood criteria are used to judge performance.
- Clear and meaningful targets, standards and measures are used to reflect the criteria.
- Employees and their managers can easily monitor performance against the specified targets.

- Employees expect that effective performance or specified behaviours will lead to a reward which they view as worthwhile.
- Employees have enough freedom to change their performance by altering their behaviour.
- The reward is appropriate to the type of work, the people employed and to the culture of the organisation.
- There is some stability in work flows and methods.
- The reward scheme is properly designed, implemented and maintained.
- The scheme is designed to ensure that individuals cannot receive inflated rewards unrelated to their performance.
- The scheme is designed to achieve an appropriate balance between reward and paybill management.
- Employees are involved in the development and operation of the scheme.
- If the principle of performance payment is introduced it should be applied to all employees.

The list of conditions, which could be extended further, is extensive and leads to the inevitable conclusion that PRP, in whatever form it takes, is very difficult to manage well, and unless a local authority is prepared to invest the necessary time, effort and skill in managing it, it is probably best avoided.

Recent developments

Competency frameworks

There has been something of a rush to embrace the term 'competency' in recent years despite the fact that there is some ambiguity in its usage. Promoted initially in the context of teaching and training it signified a move away from transferring knowledge to a situation where students and trainees were taught and tested in relation to their ability 'to do the job' rather than just knowing how it should be done. It has been very successfully applied in the workplace in relation to those jobs and tasks that are easily defined in terms of both the process involved and the expected outcome or results. The system of National Vocational Qualifications (NVQs) developed in recent years is based on competencies and has had an enormous impact on the way people are now trained, particularly in those areas of work where few staff have traditionally received formal training or obtained qualifications (e.g. domiciliary and residential care assistants in Social Services). Some local authorities have used the competencies built into NVQs as a basis for recruiting, for job specifications and for their internal training programmes.

NVQs have contributed significantly to developing the competency of those employed in lower paid jobs and, because of their progressive structure, have provided stepping-stones for learning and for job progression.

The growth in the use of management competencies was stimulated by the publication of two major reports in 1987 by Handy and by Constable and McCormick, both of which identified considerable deficiencies in the training and development of managers in the UK. Following these reports, the National Forum for Management Education and Training was launched with the Management Charter Initiative (MCI) as its operational arm.

The most visible and influential output of the MCI has been its development and publication of the competency based National Standards for Managers (MCI, 1995). The development of the standards for supervisory, first-line and middle managers was achieved relatively quickly but the identification of competencies for senior management was slower because greater difficulty was experienced in reaching agreement on what senior managers do, what contribution they make to their organisations and what competencies they therefore need to possess. In addition, the view was put forward that competencies, particularly at the senior management level, even where they can be defined, are contextually specific, relating to particular organisations and even to particular jobs at specific times. This argument was supported by Sparrow and Boam (1992) who suggested that competencies are related to organisational life cycles and environments and that they therefore have their own life cycles. Some competencies may be regarded as 'core' ones having an enduring relevance. Others are emergent – becoming increasingly significant. Yet others may be regarded as transient – important only as an organisation progresses through a particular point in its lifecycle or during particular types of organisational change. Finally there are the competencies that may be regarded as maturing and becoming less relevant.

This contextual approach has considerable relevance for local government as it moves into a further period of change stimulated by the government. Best Value will create the need for new competencies for managers and councillors and some existing ones will need to be developed and given greater prominence . Redefining the role of local government by giving greater prominence to 'community governance' and 'community leadership' roles, or by contributing to the concept of democratic renewal will also create the need for a re-prioritisation of some competencies and the development of new ones. The approach is reflected in an attempt by the Society of Chief Executives (SOLACE) to define a set of competencies required for 'community planning and engagement.' (Rogers and SOLACE, 1998). The framework produced demonstrates that councillors and front-line staff, as well as managers, will need to possess and demonstrate competencies that have not always been highly valued or demonstrated.

In a broader context, Virtanen (1996), working from the viewpoint of a European-wide definition of the 'New Public Management', has proposed a framework of new competencies specific to the public sector based on four main areas, each of which have value and instrumental components.

- **Ethical competence** – referring to conformance to a set of prevailing moral values and norms and their demonstration through processes of ethical justification and argument.
- **Political competence** – referring to the ideology and interests of public managers and to the legitimisation of their use of power.
- **Professional competence** – referring to their control of the development of policies and services and the development of 'professional' skills in implementation, administration, and co-operation.
- **Task competence** – referring to both the motivation and the ability to undertake specific tasks. (Virtanen, 1996)

Virtanen's conclusion that competencies are in transition as the role of the public sector is continuously transformed raises doubts about the validity of competency frameworks that purport to be of universal and lasting applicability. A number of local authorities have enthusiastically adopted universal frameworks such as the MCI's although a proportion have followed the practice of private sector firms, such as Cadbury Schweppes and BP, in customising the framework to provide a better 'goodness-of-fit' with the organisation. But whether the frameworks used are local or national their most important characteristics are that, first they must be dynamic rather than static, thereby avoiding the risk of becoming outdated and irrelevant, and second, they must have a built-in developmental capacity so that individuals can progressively develop their competencies from a low to a high level.

The balanced scorecard

The concept of a 'balanced scorecard' was introduced by Kaplan and Norton (1996) as a means of overcoming the tendency in the private sector to give undue or exclusive prominence to financially based indicators of performance. Introduced initially as a comprehensive framework for analysing organisational performance, it has been used by several local authorities for evaluating performance. It was, for example, adapted by Birmingham City Council as a way of overcoming the problem it was experiencing with its initial approach to the content of performance contracts for chief and other senior officers. The annual contracts were considered to be too narrow and failed to focus on the personal role of the officers in contributing to the most significant aspects of corporate and departmental performance. They therefore used an adapted form of the balanced scorecard as a means of ensuring a clearer and more balanced focus on each officer's contribution to each of the main dimensions of the scorecard (see Figure 7. 8). A limited number of objectives were specified in each of the 5 dimensions and these have in practice been a mixture of personal and departmental objectives. In addition there continue to be a small number of general management objectives that relate to corporate objectives in areas such as financial management, human resource management, equal opportunities and the development of a more corporate approach. The approach has also, by focusing on the five key areas of performance, assisted in developing joint objectives in those areas of policy, such as the development of a youth strategy, that require cross-departmental working.

Appraisal in the round

Three new developments can be identified:

- upwards appraisal
- peer appraisal or review
- 360 degree review.

Upwards appraisal

Most appraisal schemes are established on the principle that they create a dialogue between appraisee and appraiser but the hierarchical nature of relationships in local authorities has meant that in practice the dialogue often becomes top-down rather than two-way. In order to overcome the limitations of this style of appraisal some local authorities have built into their procedures specific requirements for appraisees to be able to comment on the way in which their manager's behaviour affects the way they are able to perform. Other authorities, perhaps realising that such an approach would be insufficient to counteract the dominant hierarchical basis of the appraisal process, have introduced separate but complementary processes of upwards appraisal.

Peer appraisal or review

Systems of peer appraisal were originally developed for those staff who did not form part of a clear management hierarchy or who were at the top of the

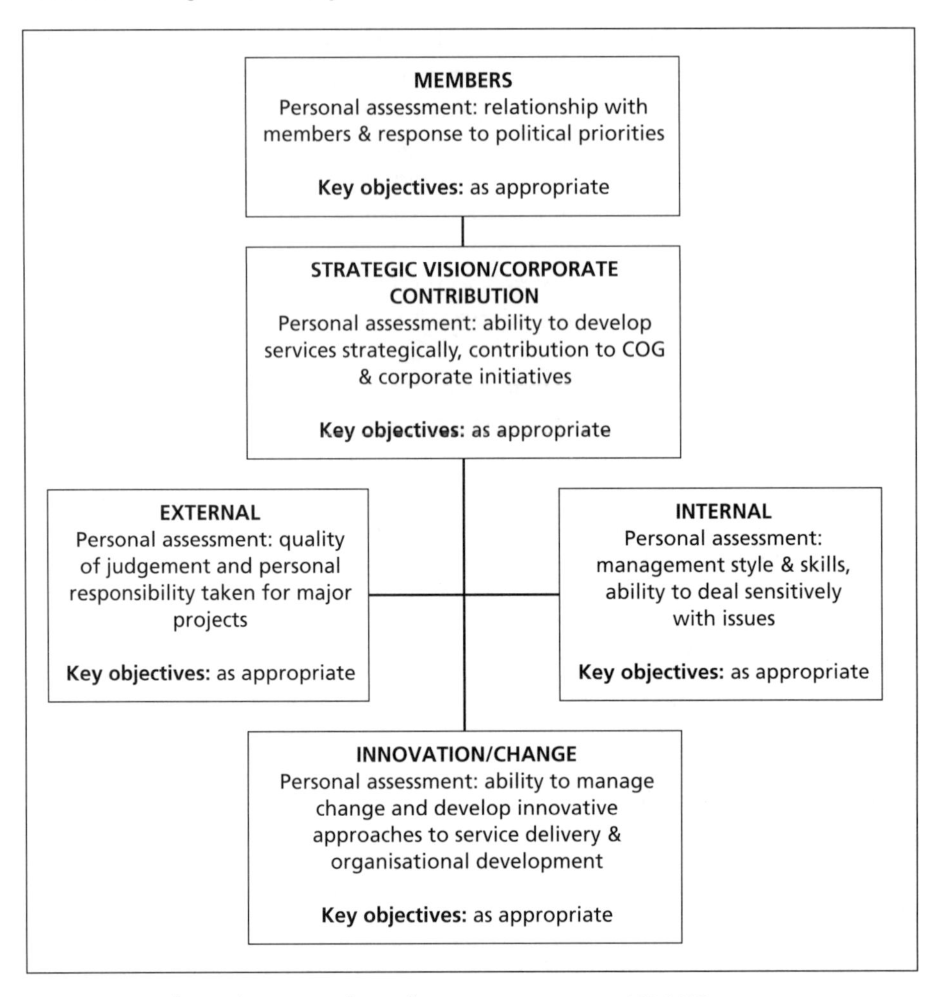

Figure 7.8 Balanced scorecard: performance contracts 1994/95

Source: Birmingham City Council

hierarchy. Peer review systems have been developed for consultants in the NHS and for head teachers in schools. Although some interest has been shown in the concept, the author has found only limited evidence of its more general use in local government, primarily for some professional posts in departments of legal services and social services.

360 degree review

Interest in the idea of obtaining a wider, more complete range of feedback to staff was stimulated by the growth of systems developed by occupational psychologists and by the development of the 'Synchrony' methodology by the Local Government Management Board for its Top Managers Programme. These systems vary in the criteria of performance or competencies they use but all are based on the concept of obtaining feedback for an individual from line managers, colleagues, staff and even suppliers and customers – thereby creating the full 360 degree picture – as illustrated in Figure 7.9.

Some local authorities have used one of the many commercial products available, such as Crewe and Nantwich's use of the Centre for Creative Leadership's benchmarked 360 degree feedback process. Others, such as Dorset County Council, have developed the capacity to operate a similar process themselves. Called 'Upward Feedback', it focuses on an individual manager and is carefully structured using questionnaires completed by the manager, her/his boss and a number of her/his staff. The questionnaires are analysed independently and the results fed back to the manager who can then discuss them with other managers and/or a facilitator and then with her/his staff. The process provides a structured opportunity for staff to share their perceptions of how their managers are fulfilling their roles.

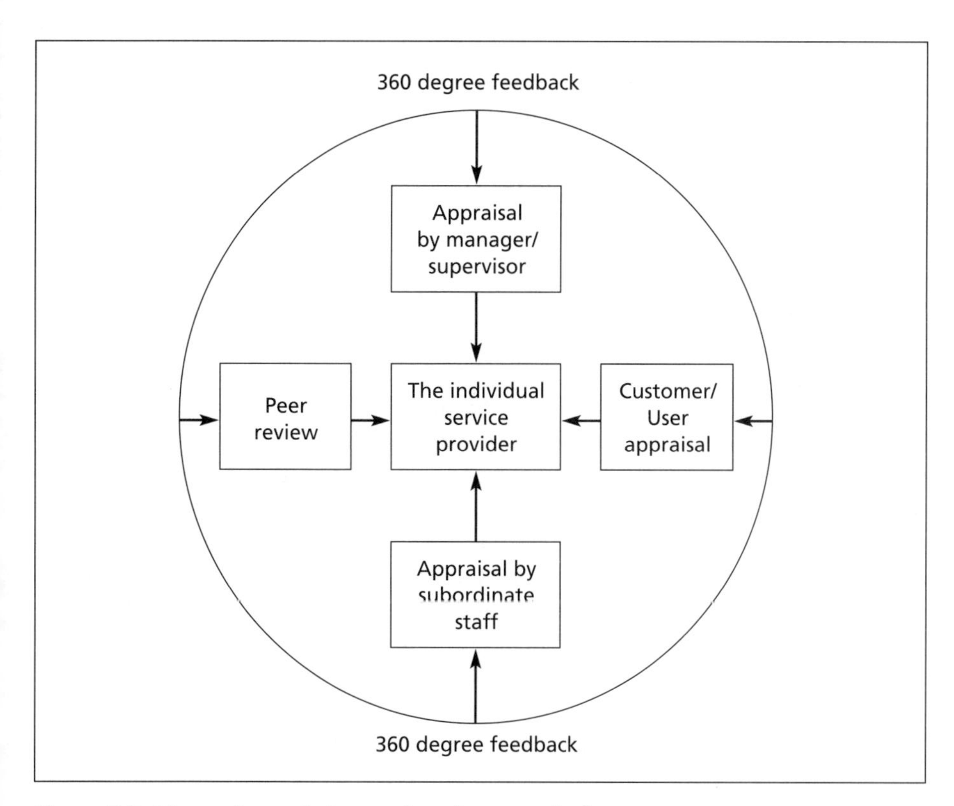

Figure 7.9 The variety of view points for appraisal

360 degree review has been used with some success in local government, primarily for senior managers, but, because it is relatively time-consuming and costly, it is likely to remain something which is used selectively to supplement rather than to replace the more traditional form of one-to-one appraisal.

Coaching and counselling

Some local authorities have complemented their appraisal processes by providing training for managers in how they can provide coaching and counselling for their staff in order to overcome the performance problems identified in the appraisal process. Others have developed specialists who can support managers and their staff in dealing with problems such as stress or in designing personal development action plans. Some, such as Flintshire, have a more widely based occupational health unit that can deal with a variety of problems. In other local authorities, increased delegation to unit managers and the stripping out of corporate support services as part of organisational rationalisation and delayering processes has left many managers without the skills, support, and sometimes the resources, to deal effectively with certain kinds of performance problems. It is increasingly recognised, however, that it may be inappropriate and even dangerous for individual managers to seek to resolve certain kinds of psychological and behavioural problems. In either rationalising and/or decentralising, local authorities must ensure that their managers really are 'empowered' to resolve performance problems in the workplace.

Conclusion

All systems for appraising and managing human behaviour are imperfect because our understanding, theoretically and practically, of how to influence behaviour is imperfect. In addition, such systems raise ethical questions relating to the boundary between justified 'management' and unjustifiable 'manipulation'. Despite their imperfections, such systems are needed not just so that organisations can work effectively towards achieving their objectives but so that their employees can be treated and judged with some degree of equity and fairness. Appraisal, in one form or another, is likely to remain a key tool of performance management and hopefully local authorities will find ways of making it a dynamic and real part of the management process rather than a bureaucratic form-filling exercise. The current interest in new forms of appraisal suggests that this can be achieved.

8

Politics and performance – the role of councillors in reviewing performance

Introduction

The purpose of this chapter is to explore ways in which councillors can play a more effective part in monitoring and reviewing policy and performance by exploring changing ideas and practices in relation to committee structures, decision-making processes and the roles and skills of councillors.

In recent years, local authorities have shown a greater capacity to be innovatory in their management practices than in their democratic practices. The many changes in the roles and expectations of officers have contrasted with the relative stability that has existed for councillors. In some authorities, reform of the political process has been limited to occasional tinkering with the committee structure whilst keeping it firmly rooted in traditional concepts of service committees that give emphasis to one, limited view of the role of councillors.

The relative lack of change has not been for want of advice. Repeated recommendations for change have been directed at creating more streamlined committee systems, a more executive style of decision making, and a greater scrutiny and review role for councillors. Proposals for reform and improvement can be traced through a series of major reports that include the Maud Report (1967), the Bains Report (1972), the Widdicombe Committee Report on the conduct of local authority business (1986), and the Department of the Environment Working Party's consultative paper (1991) and report (1993) on the internal management of local authorities. The consultative paper, in seeking to promote more effective and speedy decision making, the enhanced scrutiny of services, and the devotion by more councillors of more time to their constituency role, suggested a number of options which included: the adaptation of the committee system; a cabinet system; the appointment of Council Managers; and directly elected mayors. There were also several reports published by the Audit Commission, including 'We Can't Go On Meeting Like This' (1991), in which the Commission questioned the amount of time taken up by council committees and the tendency for committees to concentrate on issues of operational management rather than strategy and review.

The relative lack of change that has resulted from these reports may be ascribed to four factors.

- Some of the reports gave insufficient recognition to how councillors actually carry out and view their role, thereby resulting in a perceived lack of relevance to many councillors. Recommendations that were not grounded in the experience and expectations of councillors were, not surprisingly, largely ineffective.
- Councillors have been cautious and conservative in reconsidering their role despite the fact that many of them found cause for dissatisfaction with the traditional committee process.
- There were constraints on radical change imposed by the legal framework.
- The lack of clear models that adequately reflect the multiple and sometimes conflicting roles which councillors are required to perform.

Applying commercial models of governance, in which councillors are likened to the board of directors or parliamentary models, can be difficult. Other models, based on managerial processes such as that contained in Figure 8.1, whilst being of relevance to an authority generally, have not helped clarify what the role of the councillor should be in the process. There has been a tendency to assume that councillors can be slotted into such managerial models with little real consideration of the relationship between the political and managerial processes.

But there has been some change, albeit within the constraints imposed by the legal framework. In recent years there appears to have been a greater preparedness not only to restructure the committee system but also to engage in a greater variety of decision-making processes and arenas. These changes appear in some councils to have followed a fundamental management reorganisation but in others have resulted from a recognition of the need to fundamentally reconsider the way in which local democracy works.

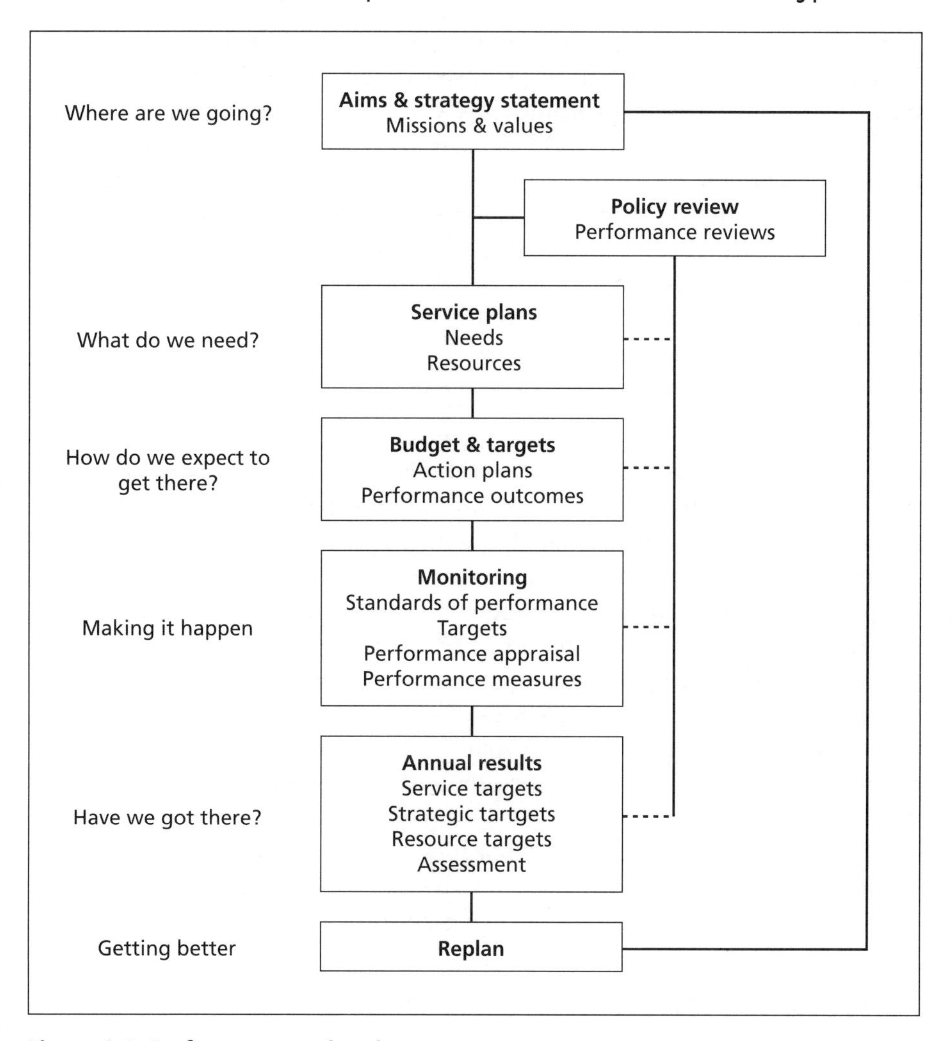

Figure 8.1 Performance review in context

Source: Association of District Councils – Performance Review Guide for Elected Members, 1991

The current debate and proposals

In recent years there has been an even more rapid flow of reports including: the Commission for Local Democracy (1995); the Audit Commission's 'Representing The People' (1997); the report of the Nolan Committee on standards of conduct in local government (1997); and the government's three Green Papers on Best Value, Local Democracy and Community Leadership, and a New Ethical Framework (DETR 1998a,b,c). The current DETR Green

Paper 'Local Democracy and Community Leadership', in a section entitled 'Modernising the way councils work', picks up the Audit Commission's theme that councillors are overburdened by a committee structure that is 'inefficient and opaque' (DETR, 1998c) and invites views about the possible introduction of new decision-making models such as formal single party advisory or executive committees, lead member systems, cabinet systems and executive mayors. The 'New Ethical Framework' Green Paper (DETR, 1998b) takes as its starting point the third report of the Nolan Committee on Standards in Public Life (Nolan Committee, 1997) and proposes a new framework in which all authorities would be required to introduce their own code of conduct for councillors based on a new national code and to establish a Standards Committee.

Concern for probity, ethics and the need for better corporate governance has not been limited to the public sector. A series of well publicised company failures and ensuing scandals together with public concern at the level of top executives' pay in the newly privatised utility companies, led to the appointment of the Cadbury Committee on the financial aspects of corporate governance. The Committee's report in 1996 made effective internal control a key factor of good corporate governance, central to which was the concept of an audit committee. Although the idea of audit committees has been proposed and supported by some groups in local government, the government did not make a specific proposal for their introduction. Finally, the 'Best Value' Green Paper (DETR, 1997a), discussed in greater detail in Chapter 3, contains a number of implications for the role of councillors (rather than for the committee structure) by placing much greater emphasis on their role in monitoring and reviewing performance.

Performance review

The involvement of councillors in reviewing performance has been a source of almost continuous debate and advice since the Bains Committee in 1972 made its recommendation that every local authority should have a performance review sub-committee. The Audit Commission has also stressed the importance of councillors having a full and significant role in reviewing performance and, in its advice during the 1980s, strongly recommended the use of performance review committees or sub-committees. In the 1990s it appeared to be less certain that such committees were necessary and instead the Commission stressed the need for clear processes rather than particular organisational arrangements (see Audit Commission, 1989, 1990 and 1997). The Department of the Environment Working Party Report (1993) recommended that the local authority associations should commission written material from local authorities on, *inter alia*, the establishment of committees to scrutinise and review policy formulation and performance.

Despite the repeated demands for councillors to become more closely involved in monitoring and reviewing performance and despite repeated attempts to bring this about, it does not appear to be an area of political activity that has met with a great deal of success. Councillors and officers frequently experience a sense of frustration which is evidenced by the following comments made by councillors from a variety of councils.

> *'There is no culture of review amongst officers or members.'*
>
> *'We lack a clearly defined corporate view on which to base our reviews.'*
>
> *'There is a lack of any strong corporate strategy which would provide both the framework and focus for performance review within service committees.'*
>
> *'The only formal review we have is as part of the departmental annual reports to committees which are so vague as to be invisible.'*
>
> *'The role of the Performance Review Sub-Committee creates a risk of conflict with service committees – with the consequence that its role is restricted to monitoring paper clips.'*
>
> *'The Performance Review Committee is a talking shop rather than a review body.'*
>
> *'There is a lack of understanding by members. Officers always set the agenda.'*
>
> *'Members lack interest – there is not enough questioning.'*
>
> *'There are too many figures and not enough questioning.'*
>
> *'We used to have a Performance Review Sub-Committee but it was toothless and councillors did not want to serve on it'.*

The quotations from councillors attending the author's seminars in recent years, reflect some of the problems involved in creating a meaningful role for councillors in reviewing performance – a role which is nonetheless perceived as potentially important by many councillors and officers. The remainder of this chapter explores four of the problems: committee structures; decision-making processes; political and organisational culture; and the skills required of councillors.

Committee structures

The way in which performance monitoring and review is located in the committee structure remains an important issue and it is clear that local authorities are experimenting with a number of options beyond the Bains' concept of a single performance review sub-committee reporting to the policy committee. It is important to recognise that certain principles, set out below, have to be considered when determining the most appropriate organisational location.

- **Independence versus integration** – one of the repeated arguments for having a separate performance review body is that it should be **independent** of the executive decision-making process conducted in the council and in service committees so that it can act as an effective scrutineer of decision making and implementation. Comparisons are often made with the Public Accounts Committee or select committees in Parliament. The purpose of such committees in the parliamentary context is that they act as a formal check by the legislature (i.e. Parliament) on the political executive (i.e. the government). While there is a strong case, in terms of good democratic government, for local authorities to have similar arrangements, it is difficult to replicate them in practice because there is no formal distinction between executive and legislature – all councillors are members of the executive. This makes it difficult for a councillor to act in the independent way that is theoretically possible for a backbench member of the House of Commons. The second argument for the 'independence' concept concerns the clarity of perception and analysis which someone coming afresh to a problem or issue can apply – frequently expressed colloquially as 'seeing the wood from the trees'.

  The case for **integration** is a more managerial one and is associated with a view of accountability that demands that those who are responsible for making decisions should also be responsible for the consequences and results of their decisions. The issue is to find ways, structural and procedural, whereby all levels of the decision-making process, from strategy to detailed implementation, are as integrated as possible.

  It is evident that the two concepts, one based on good government and the other on good management, do not fit easily together and many of the problems experienced by local authorities may be attributed to their attempt to serve both concepts.

- **Alignment versus cross-cutting** – any form of separate performance review body may either be closely aligned with the main committee system or it may cut across the boundaries that the committee structure creates. A local authority organised on a service committee basis will tend to be dominated by a service perspective while a council organised on an area committee basis will be dominated by a geographical perspective. Performance review may be organised so that it reflects that dominant perspective or so that it deliberately provides a counter-perspective.

  The case for alignment is a strong one because the main decision-making processes and the documentation and information systems that underpin them will be unified, thereby making monitoring and review easier. There is also a strong case for performance review providing a cross-cutting perspective, be it geographical, client group or issue based. By ensuring that the perspectives of different stakeholder groups are incorporated in the review process, local democracy can be enhanced. The case against a cross-cutting perspective is that it is more difficult to achieve and, even where it is carried out, it may be more difficult to ensure that it has a real impact on the prevailing perspective. All local authorities are faced with deciding whether to use simple, uni-dimensional structures and processes, which may be attractive in terms of their operational practicality, or more complex, matrix structures and processes that seek to give a voice to alternative perspectives. Current management thinking has stressed the need for simple structures and processes because they create clearer lines of internal accountability. That is their strength. Their weakness is that they do not adequately reflect the real complexity of community governance.

In broad terms there are five ways in which a local authority can locate the performance review function within its committee structure, four of which are illustrated in Figure 8.2.

Model 1: the independent committee – an accountability model

This model stresses the achievement of accountability by means of an independent scrutiny of policy making and performance. The model is based upon the parliamentary concept of a legislative check on the executive.

For an independent committee to work, certain conditions need to be fulfilled.

- Reports of the committee should be published on a regular basis and made widely available because the committee is the public face of the local authority's accountability mechanisms.
- The independence of the committee needs to be ensured and preserved by providing it with clear terms of reference, including the right to explore any issues it considers appropriate, and by providing it with clear access to any information it requires. Reporting relationships also need to be clarified; the committee should be given the freedom to report to the full council on either a regular basis or as it thinks fit.
- The method of working needs to be made clear and it is likely that procedures will need to be relatively formal with clear definitions of the focus and purpose of each review, the investigative approach to be used and the extent of the committee's freedom to call on evidence from organisations and individuals outside the authority.
- The membership of the committee should be drawn from backbench councillors.

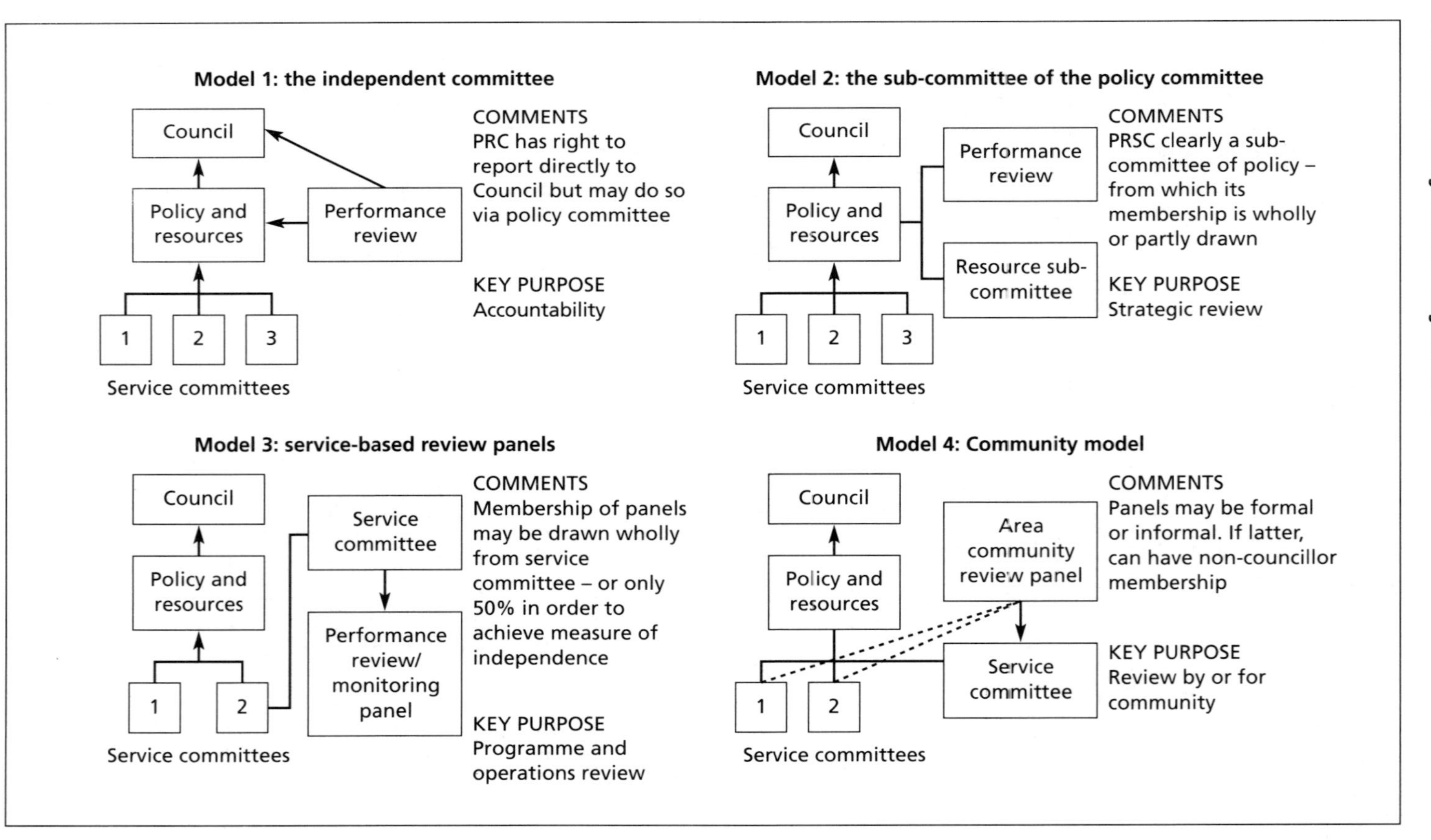

Figure 8.2 Performance review – organisational arrangements

There appear to be few examples of authorities adopting this model, although some have claimed to do so. Real independence is hard to achieve and the formality of process required may also create problems. There is a stark contrast between the formality of an independent scrutiny, with its demands for public hearing, formal process and clarification of the rights of those who may be called before it, and the more informal probing, questioning approach which is likely to produce a less confrontational and more collaborative approach to improving performance and overcoming difficult performance problems. In the words of one councillor:

> *Genuine scrutiny is reflective and best conducted through discursive, almost conversational, probing. A large public committee is perhaps the wrong place for this to be done.*

Model 2: the sub-committee of policy – a strategic review model

This model was recommended by the Bains Committee (1972) and is one which has been adopted by many local authorities. The logic of having performance review conducted by a sub-committee of the policy and resources committee is that it has delegated to it responsibility for the strategic review of key policy issues but in practice many sub-committees of this kind have attempted to carry out a comprehensive review of the performance rather than a selective review of policy. This often results in the sub-committee becoming overburdened and its reviews superficial. To avoid this, such sub-committees need to adopt a much more selective approach limited either to a review of key policies or to a few, in depth analyses of selected aspects of performance. Some authorities, such as Kent County Council, adopted the idea of reviewing 20 per cent or 25 per cent of the authority's services or policies each year, an approach that is now proposed as part of the Best Value process.

Model 3: service-based reviews – an integrated model

The creation of a sub-committee or panel for all or some of the main committees, although not yet widespread, appears to be becoming more popular. The development of performance management systems has meant that many service committees have developed a more extensive role in monitoring and reviewing performance and have in some cases delegated all or some of this task to a standing sub-committee, panel or working group. The advantage of this approach is that it enables a clear focus on performance monitoring to be achieved. Monitoring and review are not squeezed in at the end of a long agenda. In addition it has provided an opportunity for councillors who want to specialise in review to develop specialist skills and knowledge. The danger inherent in this approach is that it may appear to absolve the main committee of responsibility. One way of overcoming this problem is by ensuring that the main committee remains responsible for the regular and systematic monitoring of operational performance and an annual general review of strategies and policies while the sub-committee has delegated to it the conduct of in-depth investigations of particular policy or performance issues identified by the main committee.

There are now numerous examples of this approach. South Hams District Council created member Review Groups for each main committee that investigate, analyse and make recommendations to their parent committees. In Stevenage all main committees created Performance and Quality Working Committees that reported twice yearly on performance generally and also carried out selected in-depth reviews. Salford City Council, as part of a major structural review considered the creation of Quality and Performance Review panels for each main committee. In some local authorities a more selective approach has been adopted with only some service committees having a performance review panel. Warwickshire County Council, for example, just has a panel for its Education Committee.

A separate sub-committee or panel is not however a prerequisite of successful service based performance review. There are several examples of service committees carrying out their own responsibilities for monitoring and review in a rigorous and systematic manner. In Epsom and Ewell Borough Council a well-developed performance management and review system is an integral aspect of the way the authority is managed. The core part of the monitoring and review carried out by councillors is conducted in the service committees by means of:

- regular reports from cost centre managers on performance against specified performance indicators;
- annual service reports;
- the involvement of users in service reviews using a variety of user groups, panels and forums;
- analysis of community polls which assess satisfaction levels.

Model 4: area and neighbourhood panels – a community perspective model

There are an increasing number of local authorities that have adopted some form of geographical perspective through the creation of a variety of area, neighbourhood or community based sub-committees, panels or forums.

While the responsibility of these bodies is rarely stated explicitly as being to monitor and review performance, in practice this is what a number of them do. They have an important function of providing a community perspective to monitoring and review.

Some authorities, such as South Somerset District Council and the London Borough of Tower Hamlets (during its period of Liberal Democrat control), have adopted a radical approach by making areas or neighbourhoods the dominant perspective for the committee structure. Other authorities have been less radical but have nonetheless sought to introduce a geographical perspective. Nottinghamshire County Council established panels for three areas of the county within its community services committee. Each panel had a remit to scrutinise a number of cross-service reviews. North Kesteven District Council has carried out community audits of rural parishes involving an analysis of the characteristics of the parish, a SWOT analysis carried out by the parish council and community leaders, and the production of a vision statement. This was followed by a consultative draft action plan which led to the implementation of specific programmes and projects. Sheffield set up monitoring groups in six areas covering the city and York is one of several authorities that has set up neighbourhood forums throughout its area. Many other authorities of all types and sizes have introduced not dissimilar arrangements (see Stewart, 1996 for further examples).

Model 5 – policy, client or issue review panels – a cross-cutting issues model

This model, not illustrated in Figure 8.2, represents another limited but growing trend for local authorities to create permanent or ad hoc panels that focus on individual issues, areas of policy or client groups. For example, in Coventry policy teams were created that were responsible for co-ordinating broadly defined areas of policy. In Arun, prior to the elections in May 1995, four workshop groups were created to look at the key issues of people, jobs, homes and environment. In the London Borough of Bexley four advisory committees were created to help develop comprehensive and consistent policies for particular issues and client groups. Cambridgeshire County Council introduced select panels that operated within a specific time defined by the policy committee. The subject for each panel was determined by the party groups and topics included economic development, people at risk, road safety, deprivation and disadvantage.

In all these examples, while the major purpose of the panels may not be to monitor and review performance, some aspect of their work inevitably involves those functions and in all cases provides an opportunity for the council to inject a different perspective in re-evaluating both policy and performance.

Roles for performance review committees and sub-committees

Performance review bodies, whatever their location in the committee structure, appear in practice to have a variety of roles. The author's own research, carried out over a number of years, has identified at least 12 different roles.

- **Monitoring the authority's own performance management and review systems and procedures**.
- **Strategic policy review** – reviews in this category are normally highly selective but may be wide-ranging in those cases where strategic development involves a number of service committees and departments.
- **Comprehensive review** – corporate performance review bodies may be set up with the responsibility for reviewing all aspects of the authority's activities. It is an approach that often results in councillors submerging in a sea of service and business plans and reports. Problems may also result from the need to spread the review process throughout the year whereas the needs of the authority may demand that reviews of each service are carried out as soon as possible after the end of the financial year so that any changes can be fed into the following year's policy and budgetary cycle. This comprehensive approach tends to result in a fairly superficial review which has little impact on either policy or performance. It may at best have a symbolic purpose in demonstrating that the authority is at least going through the motions of reviewing all its services.
- **Independent reviews** – some performance review bodies are set up with wide-ranging terms of reference and the remit to select whatever issues or services for review that they think fit. Such bodies can become marginalised and exhibit a tendency to pursue the particular interests of the councillors who happen to be members rather than the wider interests of the council. Where however they involve service users and community representatives in their deliberations they can serve a useful role.
- **Cross-cutting and 'wicked issues' reviews** – in these cases the role of the performance review body is specifically focused on those aspects of policy and/or performance which cross over the main organisational boundaries of the authority.

- **Management of a policy and review unit** – there have been one or two examples where the performance review body has been made responsible for the management of the officer units, such as policy and performance review or research and development. In effect the body becomes a service committee and its attention is diverted from the review process to the concerns of the support unit. This is not a recommended role.
- **A corporate focus for value for money or quality improvement programmes** – many authorities, particularly when the effects of tighter budgetary controls imposed by the government were first experienced, set up committees or panels to play a central role in providing authority-wide councillor involvement in budgetary reviews. In more recent years it remains not uncommon for the concept of performance review to be equated with that of value for money, or more recently with the concept of quality, resulting in the emergence of 'quality and performance review' committees, panels and working parties.
- **Monitoring and review of the capital programme** – a few performance review bodies were given a particular responsibility for monitoring and evaluating the authority's capital programme during the 1970s and 1980s but with the general reduction in capital expenditure less emphasis now appears to be given to this activity.
- **A customer focus** – the provision of a corporate focus for monitoring and reviewing strategies for improving customer service has been an important element of some performance review bodies.
- **Complaints monitoring and review** – this can be an important function in an authority wishing to develop its complaints procedures. An authority-wide analysis of the pattern and trends of complaints can be very revealing and can provide an important supplement to the monitoring of individual complaints.
- **Citizens Charter performance indicators** – this involves responsibility for overseeing the publication of, and the public's response to, the indicators as well as a corporate oversight of the levels of performance recorded and the encouragement of the use of benchmarking.
- **Consideration of the auditor's management letter and Audit Commission studies**.

Decision-making processes

In this context the word 'processes' refers to both the level and type of review which is carried out and the scope of that review. It is important for councillors to distinguish between the different types of review that can be carried out so that they can clarify the purpose of individual reviews and decide where responsibility should be allocated within the committee structure. One categorisation of different levels of review has been provided by the Public Administration Research Centre (1988). Five levels of review were identified.

- *Operations review* – a detailed analysis of an individual operational unit examining the costs, tasks and methods used.
- *Contract review* – the monitoring and review of a contractor's performance by a client. This kind of review may include an examination of internal contracts or service level agreements.
- *Service review* – an analysis of the performance of a particular service or department.
- *Policy review* – a review of the policies, objectives and key targets which have previously been set.
- *Strategic review* – a systematic review of the environmental changes which affect the local authority and its area and an assessment of the implications of those changes for the strategies, policies and performance of the local authority.

The main questions that this classification raises for councillors are which levels of review should they be directly involved in and which should they ensure are being carried out by their officers? In practice, many reviews take place at levels one and two but it is questionable whether this is the most valuable use of councillors' time and it may be argued that councillors should focus more of their attention on levels three, four and five. The classification can be reduced to three fundamental types of review.

- **Operational performance reviews** – which take place within predetermined policy or contract requirements. Such reviews may also be called **implementation reviews**.
- **Policy reviews** – which question the appropriateness of previously set policy or contract specifications and which may lead to a restatement of either policy or contract.
- **Reviews of the external environment** – which are not in themselves reviews of the authority's own policies and performance, but may lead to some change in policy.

The distinction between policy reviews and performance reviews is readily understood but, while many performance review bodies apparently have the right to conduct reviews of policy, because of political and organisational defensiveness, they may in practice be limited to reviews of operational performance. The distinction between these levels and types of reviews is reflected most clearly in authorities such as Kirklees Metropolitan District Council where, following a wide-ranging review of the committee structure and of the representative role of councillors, four types of scrutiny and review were identified: performance review, policy review, quality review and scrutiny commissions.

Performance review

Performance review in Kirklees has the purpose of keeping 'the whole activity of a service under constant review by regularly reporting to members some objective information about what the service is doing.' The reviews are supported by an annual service planning process which sets out objectives for the year, specifies the revenue, capital and staffing budgets and provides key indicators of service performance. Performance against service plans is regularly reported to committees and monitoring of financial and personnel data is carried out by a resources sub-committee with the policy committee also monitoring performance against the Citizens Charter performance indicators.

Policy review

Policy review provides 'an in depth look at a selected aspect, asking whether it is achieving members' aims or whether it is time for a fresh approach.' The aim is for each service committee to review one area of activity in each committee cycle with preparatory investigations being undertaken by small working parties and with each committee being required to determine an annual programme of reviews for approval by the policy committee.

Quality review

Quality review is intended 'to provide feedback on the service from the standpoint of the user's actual experience.' These reviews are undertaken by councillors visiting facilities, meeting customers and the staff who deliver services and who report back to their service committees.

Scrutiny commissions

Scrutiny commissions form the most novel part of the Kirklees proposals although there have been similar developments in a number of other local authorities (see below). In Kirklees the purpose of the scrutiny commissions is 'to investigate any issue which has an impact on the public of Kirklees and to lead public debate.' The political groups on the council nominate topics for scrutiny to the policy committee which then defines the terms of reference for each commission and appoints members to it. Officers prepare background information and the commissions hold public hearings before drawing up a final report to the council.

Public scrutiny and quango watch panels

The concept of public scrutiny of either the council's own services or of other public service organisations has been developed in a number of ways. In the London Borough of Haringey a formal process of service quality review was instituted in 1995 involving four stages. First, the public and service users are invited to a meeting where a small number of user representatives deliver reports which are discussed and further contributions are encouraged from the members of the public present. Officers from the service under scrutiny are then committed to drawing up an action plan within three months which addresses the complaints raised and utilises the suggestions of users for service improvements. At a second public meeting user representatives and councillors scrutinise the action plan in detail with the aim of assessing how realistic it is. After a period of one year a third public meeting is held which scrutinises progress made against the standards and targets set. (Carey, 1995)

The London Borough of Bromley has set up a public services forum to scrutinise issues which concern local citizens and which involve the responsibilities of at least one other organisation involved in the provision of public services. Stevenage has created a local monitoring sub-committee terms of reference that include monitoring:

> *the policies of unelected public sector bodies and the services they provide, considering the implications of their policies for the Stevenage community, canvassing the opinions of the community on the services and policies, providing information to the community about the work of these bodies and responding to their consultations on policy developments. (Quoted in Stewart, 1996)*

Bristol City Council's performance review sub-committee, as part of the Council's commitment to 'the governance of Bristol', agreed a set of good practice measures as the basis for action by the Council to improve the accountability to local people of unelected public service bodies. Solihull Metropolitan Borough Council's approach emerged from the Council's concern about a single issue, the proposed closure of a hospital, but was subsequently extended.

With an increasing number of authorities recognising that their role as community leaders requires them to become involved in issues and problems beyond the delivery of their own services, it is not surprising that several scrutiny commissions or panels have been set up to scrutinise the decisions and activities of other organisations. In many respects it forms an exciting development in which authorities can give practical expression to the general concepts of community governance and leadership. But it is a development which provides both a challenge and a danger. The challenge is to find a methodology for scrutinising other organisations which does not conflict with the need for authorities to increasingly work in partnership with the organisations they are scrutinising. Scrutinies which are carried out in a conflictual or insensitive way may damage existing partnerships or prevent the development of new ones. The danger is that, in seeking to ensure that other organisations become more publicly accountable, an authority neglects its own need to be accountable. Scrutiny of other organisations should not be seen as an alternative to ensuring that the council's own policies and services are subject to appropriate monitoring and review procedures.

Culture

Several of the quotations from councillors provided earlier in the chapter indicate that one of the biggest barriers to effective performance review is the lack of an organisational and political culture that provides legitimacy to the questioning and analysis of either policy or performance. In some authorities the problem is one of organisational fragmentation in which each part of the authority sees itself as a self-contained unit and sets up barriers to protect itself from any form of external evaluation. In other authorities the cultural problem results from the existence of 'a blame culture' in which the organisation seeks to ensure that when things go wrong individuals or groups are immediately identified for blame and punishment. In such authorities, the concept of accountability becomes a negative rather than a positive force and such cultures feed on themselves by producing a downward spiral of fear, defensiveness and frustration in which any questioning of performance is seen as a threat. In such organisations, individuals, departments and committees learn to avoid or divert any such questioning. The lack of a positive performance oriented culture can occur either amongst officers or councillors – leading to frustration and poor relations on both sides. Some authorities have implemented robust performance review systems at officer level but without any real involvement or support from councillors, leading to difficulties and frustrations in implementing the results of reviews. In other authorities councillors may be active in identifying and carrying out reviews but find their activities blocked by officers who resent or fear what they consider to be excessive 'interference' in their management role. The lack of a performance culture can also occur at both officer and councillor levels, in which case it can lead to a breakdown in the internal and external accountability of the authority.

Overcoming these problems is not easy but where the problem is particularly associated with the concept of performance review a change of name and approach to the review process can help. A number of authorities have, with some success, added the word 'quality' to performance review and adopted the analytical processes and techniques associated with quality improvement. Focusing on the identification of areas of improvement, rather than using the review process simply to pass judgement on past performance, can create a new and more positive response to the process.

Councillor skills for reviewing performance

Perhaps the greatest difficulty confronting councillors in carrying out a review is to recognise that it requires a different approach. In service committees they are expected to become expert in a wide range of issues relating to a service and to demonstrate their expertise by making a wide range of executive decisions, often at relatively short notice and with varying degrees of evidence and information to support their decisions. The dominant expectation is that they should be able to rapidly master the issue or problem and make a judgement about it. There is therefore a tendency to 'rush to judgement'. Within a performance review context such an approach may be neither helpful nor appropriate. Faced with a statement of actual performance set against some predetermined target or standard the temptation may be to form an immediate judgement – performance is good, bad or satisfactory. While the forming of a judgement is necessary it cannot be considered to constitute the whole of the review process. The judgemental approach has some benefits but only if it stimulates the search for higher levels of performance. If it is a manifestation of a blame culture it is more likely that officers will become more skilled at hiding unsatisfactory aspects of performance than that councillors will become skilled at revealing them.

While judgement is at the core of reviewing performance it needs to be preceded and succeeded by other important activities, the first of which is the need to ensure that councillors are themselves satisfied that they have sufficient information about the subject of their review to make an informed judgement. But performance data rarely reveals every aspect of performance nor does it provide an explanation of the level of performance it reveals. In order to improve performance it is necessary to understand the reasons why performance is as it is. This requires councillors to question and to scrutinise the information they receive – to ask the question 'Why?' If the purpose of performance review is to improve performance, it is also necessary to go beyond the making of judgements to the identification of specific ways in which performance can be improved and the specification of action plans to ensure that improvements are put into place.

The following is a list, in general terms, of the main skills councillors need to develop for reviewing performance.

- An awareness of the context within which policies and performance take place. Such an awareness can be supported by the provision of contextual information.
- An ability to express vision – a statement of what is needed, expected or anticipated.
- An ability to translate vision into concrete terms through the definition of clear objectives and service standards and targets.
- Numeracy skills. The extensive array of performance indicators now available to councillors presumes a reasonably high level of quantitative skill. But councillors, like the community in general, possess varying levels of such skills and there is a danger that quantitative performance data may be under-utilised or even dismissed. Simply to demand high levels of numeracy is insufficient. Councillors need help in analysing and interpreting what are sometimes relatively complex sets of data and officers can play an important part in providing this. Some reports to committees appear to be written with the purpose of obscuring rather than illuminating. Several pages of undigested and indigestible statistics are unlikely to assist councillors in forming a judgement – and that, in some cases, may be their purpose.
- Perseverance and persistence. Sometimes the simplest of questions are the most difficult and take the greatest time to answer. Information may not be immediately available. Reviews can sometimes take a considerable time to complete. Improvements in performance may need to be negotiated with different groups in the organisation before they can be implemented. Where there is no culture of performance, councillors may find barriers and limits placed on their work. For all these reasons reviewing performance requires enormous perseverance and persistence.
- Questioning. If it is the art of asking questions which lies at the heart of good performance review then it is necessary to understand what constitutes a good question. While it is not very meaningful to define a set of questions which are equally applicable to every type of review, it is possible to identify some of the characteristics of questions which may be more rather than less helpful. It may be argued that questions should be:
  - *Challenging* – in the sense of acting as a stimulus to thinking and action rather than as a threat to the person being questioned.

- — *Planned* – there may be a case for intuitive, 'off-the-top-of-the-head' questions in some situations but as a general style of questioning it is unlikely to be productive. Councillors need to agree, for each review they undertake, the key or critical questions they need to have answered. By pre-planning their questions councillors will also be more able to identify where there are gaps in the information they have had reported to them.
- — *Focused* – by planning their questions councillors are more likely to be able to focus on those aspects of performance which are important and relevant and about which the council itself can do something. Some reviews become sidetracked into considering issues which are either of minor importance (the counting the paper-clips syndrome) or are beyond the competence or power of the council to act on or to influence. This is a common form of diversion.
- — *Answerable* – posing conundrums may be an enjoyable intellectual game but is unlikely to promote greater understanding of performance issues. That is not to say that councillors will not be confronted by problems of performance which may be paradoxical and contradictory but the role of performance review should be to try to unravel and clarify such difficulties rather than to compound them. By revealing aspects of performance where the authority is trying to meet competing or contradictory requirements a review can play an important role in clarifying expectations and identifying solutions.

- Recognising Catch 22s. The final skill is the ability to recognise that reviewers are sometimes faced with apparently impossible situations that have been constructed for them by someone else. A commonly constructed Catch 22 is to put barriers in the way of reviewers and then to question their performance!

Conclusion

In many ways this book has had to continuously refer to compilations of performance criteria and concepts based on a single letter of the alphabet: the three 'E's, the five 'E's or the ten 'C's. By way of an epilogue the following six 'D's are suggested as the basis for managing and reviewing performance in a democratic context.

Dialogue	With the community – continuous and pervasive – to identify issues.
Data collection	Information needs to be collected about emerging issues.
Deliberation	Councillors need to do this in order to formulate ideas and responses.
Debate	Proposals need to be formally debated, both inside and outside the authority, ensuring that the views of different stakeholders are heard.
Disputation	Is an inevitable aspect of debating many of the difficult, 'wicked' issues that local authorities have to deal with. It needs to be managed to produce a positive outcome.
Decision	Rushing to this stage, without proceeding through the previous five, can be politically fatal!

References

ACAS (Advisory, Conciliation and Arbitration Service) (1990) *Appraisal Related Pay.* London: ACAS.

Ammons, D.N. (1996) *Municipal Benchmarks – assessing local performance and establishing community standards.* London: Sage.

Anderson, G.C. (1993) *Managing performance appraisal systems.* Oxford: Blackwell.

Armstrong, M. (1993) *Managing reward systems.* Open University Press.

Arun District Council (1987) Strategy Papers and Programme Plans 1987–91 and Annual Action Plans 1989–90.

Association of District Councils (1991) *Performance Review Guide for Elected Members.* London: ADC.

Association of Metropolitan Authorities, Association of District Councils, Association of County Councils and the Local Government Management Board (Undated) *Code of Conduct for Local Government.* London: LGMB.

Audit Commission (1984) *Improving Economy, Efficiency and Effectiveness.* London: Audit Commission.

Audit Commission PRSC (1989) *Managing Services Effectively: Performance Review.* London: Audit Commission.

Audit Commission (1990) *We can't go on meeting like this: the changing role of local authority members.* London: HMSO.

Audit Commission (1994) *Read All About It.* London: Audit Commission.

Audit Commission (1995a) *Calling the Tune. Performance Management in Local Government.* London: HMSO.

Audit Commission (1995b) *Management Handbook – Paying the Piper... Calling the Tune. People, Pay and Performance in local government.* London: HMSO.

Audit Commission (1995c) *Local Authority Performance Indicators Vols. 1 and 2.* London: HMSO.

Audit Commission (1995d) *Have we got news for you.* London: Audit Commission.

Audit Commission (1997) *Representing the People: The Role of Councillors.* London: Audit Commission.

Bains Report (1972) *The New Local Authorities' Management and Structure.*

Ball, R. and Monaghan, C. (1996) 'Performance Review: The British Experience' *Local Government Studies,* 22(1), 40–58.

Barkdoll, G. (1989) letter, *Public Administration Review* 49, 295.

Bexley, London Borough of (1989) *The Business Process.*

Blair, T., Rt. Hon., MP (1998) *Leading the Way: A New Vision for Local Government.* London: Institute for Public Policy Research.

Bolton Metropolitan Borough Council (undated) *Agenda for the 90's.*

Boyne, G. (1997) 'Comparing the performance of local authorities: an evaluation of the Audit Commission indicators', *Local Government Studies,* 23.

Bradford Metropolitan District Council (1997) *Community Plan 1997–2000.*

Bramham, J. (1997) *Benchmarking for People Managers*. London: Institute of Personnel and Development.

Brent, London Borough of (1996) *Corporate Strategy and Priorities 96–98.*

British Quality Foundation (1997) *Guide to Self Assessment.* BQF.

Bromley, London Borough of (1993) *Responding to change: Serving the People even Better.*

Burgess, A.A. (1983) *Policy Planning, Implementation and Review – Synopsis of Seminar Presentation at INLOGOV.*

Cadbury Committee (1992) *The Report of The Committee on the Financial Aspects of Corporate Governance.* London: Gee & Co.

Cambridge City Council (1996) *A Community Plan for Cambridge.*

Cambridgeshire County Council (1989) *Into the 1990s.*

Cambridgeshire County Council (1996) *Performance Management Scheme, Seventh Edition.*

Camden, London Borough of (1997) *Bid for Best Value pilot status.*

Campbell, J.P. and Pritchard, R.D. (1976) 'Motivation theory in industrial and organisational psychology' in Dunnette, M.D. (ed): *Handbook of Industrial and Organisational Psychology.* Chicago: Rand-McNally.

Carey, S. (1995) 'Haringey pioneers public scrutiny of services', *Association of Metropolitan Authorities News, October.* London: AMA.

Centre for Public Services (1995) *The gender impact of CCT in local government: calculation of the national costs and savings of CCT.* Sheffield: CPS.

Centre for Public Services (1997) *Strategy for Best Value. Briefing Paper 1.* Sheffield: CPS.

Cheshire County Council (1997). Painter, A and Reynolds, C. 'Going through the change!' Joint Initiative for Community Care newsletter, Spring.

Chesterfield Borough Council (1989) *Corporate Plan 1989/90.*

Commission for Local Democracy (1995) *Taking Charge: The Rebirth of Local Democracy.* CLD.

Constable, J. and McCormick, R. (1987) *The Making of British Managers: A Report for the BIM and CBI into Management, Training, Education and Development.* London: BIM.

DETR (1997) *The 12 Principles of Best Value.* London: Department of the Environment, Transport and the Regions.

DETR (1998a) *Modernising Local Government: Improving Local Services Through Best Value.* London: Department of the Environment, Transport and the Regions.

DETR (1998b) *Modernising Local Government: A New Ethical Framework.* London: Department of the Environment, Transport and the Regions.

DETR (1998c) *Modernising Local Government: Local Democracy and Community Leadership.* London: Department of the Environment, Transport and the Regions.

Department of the Environment (1991 and 1993) *Community leadership: Unlocking the Potential* and *The Report of the Working Party on the Internal Management of Local Authorities in England and Wales.* London: HMSO.

Eccles (1991) 'The Performance management manifesto'. *Harvard Business Review,* Jan.–Feb., 131–137. Reprinted in Holloway *et al.*, op. cit.

Eichel, E. and Bender, H.E. (1984) *Performance Appraisal: A Study of Current Techniques.* New York: American Management Association.

Epsom and Ewell Borough Council (1996) *Continuous Improvement: Managing Performance at Epsom and Ewell.*

European Foundation for Quality Management see British Quality Foundation (1997).

Festinger, F. (1951) 'A theory of social comparison processes', *Human Relations,* 7, 117–140.

Filkin, G. (1997) 'Best Value for the public', *Municipal Journal.* London.

Freedland, J. (1998) 'Britain's Problem with Corruption', *The Guardian*, 4 February.

Gill, D. (1977) *Appraising Performance: Present Trends and the Next Decade.* London: Institute of Personnel Management.

Hall, D. and Stewart, J. (1997) *Citizens Juries: An Evaluation.* London: LGMB.

Handy, C. (1987) *The Making of Managers: A Report on Management, Education, Training and Development in The United States, West Germany, France, Japan and the UK.* London: NEDO.

Handy, C. (1993) *Understanding Organisations.* Harmondsworth: Penguin Books.

Harman, J. (1993) Unpublished presentation to an INLOGOV seminar on committee reorganisation in Kirklees.

Hertzberg, F. (1966) *Work and the Nature of Man.* Cleveland: World Pub. Co.

Hollis, G. (1994) *Transforming Local Government: A practical management guide to local government structuring and renewal.* Harlow: Longman.

Holloway, J., Lewis, J. and Mallory, G. (eds.) (1995) *Performance Measurement and Evaluation.* London: Sage.

Humberside County Council (1994) *Staff Development and Review Scheme.*

Institute of Personnel Management (1992) *Performance Management in the UK.* London: IPM. (See also: Society of Chief Personnel Officers (1992) *Performance Management Systems in Local Government.* London: IPM.)

Ipswich Borough Council (1997). Best Value Bid.

Jackson, P. (1993) 'Public Service Performance Evaluation: A Strategic Perspective', *Public Money and Management,* 13 (4), 9–14.

Jackson, P. (ed.) (1995) *Measures for Success in the Public Sector.* A Public Finance Foundation Reader. London: CIPFA.

James, G. (1988) *Performance Appraisal.* Work Research Unit Occasional Paper 40. London: Advisory, Conciliation and Arbitration Service.

Jenkins, S. (1997) *Accountable to None: The Tory Nationalisation of Britain.*

Kaplan, R. and Norton, D. (1996) *The Balanced Scorecard.* Harvard Business School Press.

Keenan, P. (1994) Article in *Local Government Chronicle* quoted in Lewis J. op. cit.

Kraiger, K. and Ford, J. (1985) 'A Meta Analysis of Race Effects in Performance Ratings', *Journal of Applied Psychology,* 70, 56–65.

Labour Party (1995) *Renewing Democracy, Rebuilding Communities.* London: Labour Party.

Labour Party (1996) *Rules for Local Government Labour Groups.* London: Labour Party.

LACSAB (Local Authorities' Conditions of Service Advisory Board) (1990) *Performance Related Pay in Practice. Case Studies from Local Government and Handbook on Performance Related Pay.* LACSAB.

Leach, S., Walsh, K., Game, C., Rogers, S. and Spencer, K. (1993) *The Challenge of Change.* Luton: LGMB.

Lewis, J. (1996) *The Emperor's New Clothes: Accountability and the Citizen's Charter.* Unpublished MBA Dissertation. School of Public Policy, University of Birmingham.

Lewisham, London Borough of (1995) *Strategic and Service Planning: Framework and 5 Year Timetable.*

Likierman, A. (1993) 'Performance Indicators: 20 Lessons from Managerial Use', *Public Money and Management,* Oct–Dec.

Local Government Association (1998) *Best Value: A Statement of Objectives.* London: LGA.

LGMB (Local Government Management Board) (1993) *People and Performance: The LGMB Guide to Performance Management.* Luton: LGMB.

LGMB (Local Government Management Board (1994) *Performance Management and Performance Related Pay 1993 Survey.* Luton: LGMB.

LGMB (Local Government Management Board) (1997) *How the LGMB can help...Best Value.* London: LGMB,

Locke, E.A., Shaw, K., Saari, L. and Latham, G.(1981) 'Goal Setting and Task Performance 1969–80', *Psychological Bulletin*, 90, 125–152.

Locke, E.A. and Henne, D. (1986) 'Work Motivation Theories' in Cooper, C.L. and Robertson, I. (eds.) *International Review of Industrial and Organisational Psychology.* Wiley.

Long, P. (1986) *Performance Appraisal Revisited.* London: IPM.

Longenecker, C.L. and Ludwig, D. (1990) 'Ethical Dilemmas in Performance Appraisal Revisited', *Journal of Business Ethics*, 9, 961–969. Reprinted in Holloway *et al.* (op. cit.).

MCI (Management Charter Initiative) (1995) *Management Standards Directory.* London: MCI.

Martin, S. (1998) *Bidding for Best Value: a preliminary analysis of bids for inclusion in the Best Value Pilot Programme.* Paper presented to the Public Services under Labour Conference, Cardiff University.

Maslow, A. (1954) *Motivation and Personality.* New York: Harper.

McGregor, D. (1960) *The Human Side of Enterprise.* New York: McGraw-Hill.

Mento, A. J. *et al.* (1987) 'A Meta-analytic Study of Task Performance: 1966–84', *Organisational Behaviour and Human Decision Process*, 39, 52–83.

Metcalfe, L. and Richards, S. (1987) *Improving Public Management.* London: Sage.

Meyer, H.H. *et al.* (1965) 'Split Roles in Performance Appraisal', *Harvard Business Review*, Jan–Feb, 123–129.

Miller, P. (1996) *Dilemmas of Accountability: The Limits of Accounting.* Oxford: Blackwell.

Nolan Committee (1995) The First Report of The Committee on Standards in Public Life. London: HMSO.

Nolan Committee (1997) The Third Report of The Committee on Standards in Public Life. London: HMSO.

Nutley, S. and Osborne, S.P. (1994) *The Public Sector Management Handbook.* Harlow: Longman.

Peters, T.J. and Waterman, R.H. (1982) *In Search of Excellence: Lessons from America's Best-Run Companies.* London: Harper & Row.

Pettigrew, A., Ferlie, E. and McKee, L. (1993) *Shaping Strategic Change: Making Change in Large Organisations: The Case of the NHS.* London: Sage.

Pirsig, R.M. (1974) *Zen and the Art of Motorcycle Maintenance.* London: Corgi Books.

Plunkett Foundation (1993) *Ownership Options for Local Authority Services – A Guide for Policy Makers.* Oxford: Plunkett Foundation.

Pollitt, C. (1986) 'Beyond the Managerial Model: The Case for Broadening Performance Assessment in Government and the Public Services', *Financial Accountability and Management*, 2 (3), 155–70.

Power, M. (1994) *The Audit Explosion.* Paper No.7. London: Demos. (See also Power, M. (1997) *The Audit Society. Rituals of Verification.* Oxford University Press.)

Public Administration Research Centre (1988) *Performance Review. A Note for Members and Officers.* Bolton: PARC.

Randall, G., Packard, P. and Slater, J. (1984) *Staff Appraisal.* London: IPM.

Rogers, S. (1990) *Performance Management in Local Government.* Harlow: Longman.

Rogers, S. and SOLACE (1998) *Community Planning and Engagement.* School of Public Policy, University of Birmingham.

St. Edmundsbury Borough Council (1996) *Extending Excellence by Working with Communities: Corporate plan 1995–99.*

Senge, P.M. (1993) *The Fifth Discipline.* London: Century Business.

Skinner, B.F. (1971) *Beyond Freedom and Dignity.* New York: Knopf.

Smith, P. (1993) 'Outcome-related performance indicators and organisational control in the public sector', *British Journal of Management,* 4, 135–151. Reprinted in Holloway *et al.* (op. cit.).

Southwark, London Borough of (1997) *Towards Service Excellence.*

Sparrow, P.R. and Boam, R. (1992) 'Where do we go from here?' in Boam, R. and Sparrow, P.R. (eds) *Focusing on Human Resources – A Competency-based Approach.* London: McGraw-Hill.

Stewart, V. and A. (1976 and 1977) *Tomorrow's men Today,* IPM; and *Practical Performance Appraisal.* Farnborough: Gower.

Stewart, J. (1995, 1996 and 1997) Three linked publications: *Innovations in Democratic Practice; Further Innovations in Democratic Practice* (Occasional Paper 3); *More Innovations in Democratic Practice* (Occasional Paper 9). School of Public Policy, University of Birmingham.

Stewart, J. (1996) *Reviewing Structures and Processes for Councillors.* Occasional Paper 5. School of Public Policy, University of Birmingham.

Stewart, J. and Clarke, M. (1996) *Developments in Local Government.* INLOGOV Discussion Paper. University of Birmingham.

Stewart, J. and Walsh, K. (1994) 'Performance Measurement: When Performance Can Never Finally Be Defined', *Public Money and Management,* 14 (2), 45–50.

Stewart, J. and Walsh, K. (1995) 'Performance Measurement: When Performance Can Never Finally Be Defined', in Jackson, P. (1995) op. cit.

Thomas, N. and Puffitt, R. (1997) *The Best Value Contractual Cycle.* Unpublished Paper. School of Public Policy. University of Birmingham.

Troman (1994) Information for whom...are we giving customers a good deal? *Policy and Performance Review Network Newsletter,* March.

Travers, T. (1996) 'Town Hall Turns Red', *Guardian Society Supplement,* 11 Dec., 6–7.

Virtanen, T. (1996) 'The Competencies of New Public Managers', in Farnham, D., Horton, S., Barlow, J. and Hondeghem, A. *New Public managers in Europe. Public Servants in Transition.* London: Macmillan.

Vevers, P. (1998) 'Don't Crowd the Middle Ground', *Local Government Chronicle*, 27 March, 12–13.

Vroom, V. (1964) *Work and Motivation.* New York: Wiley.

Walsh, K. (1991) *Competitive Tendering for Local Authority Services: Initial Experiences.* London: HMSO.

Walsh, K. (1992) *Quality, Surveillance and Performance Measurement.* Later published in: Riley, K.A. and Nuttall, D.L. (eds.) (1994) *Measuring Quality: Education Indicators – United Kingdom and international perspectives.* London: Falmer Press.

Walsh, K. and Davies, H. (1993) *Competition and Service: The Impact of the Local Government Act 1998.* London: HMSO.

Warwick University (1998) Information Supplied to Best Value Pilot Authorities by the evaluation team based at Warwick University.

Widdecombe Committee (1986) *Report of The Committee of Inquiry into the Conduct of Local Authority Business.* Cmmd. 9797. London: HMSO.

Index